FAIL TO LEARN

FAIL TO LEARN

A MANIFESTO FOR TRAINING GAMIFICATION

SCOTT PROVENCE

Copyright © 2020 by Scott Provence

All rights reserved.

Cover art and illustrations by Will Burrows.

No part of this book may be reproduced in any form or by any electronic or mechanical means, including information storage and retrieval systems, without written permission from the author, except for the use of brief quotations in a book review.

While the author has made every effort to provide accurate information at the time of publication, neither the publisher nor the author assumes any responsibility for errors or for changes that occur after publication. Neither the author nor the publisher shall be liable or responsible for any loss or damage allegedly arising from any information or suggestions in this book. Further, the author does not have any control over and does not assume any responsibility for third-party websites or their content.

CONTENTS

Our Manifesto — vii

INTRODUCTION
1. Welcome to the Revolution — 3
2. How Much Do You Fail and Play? — 15

I. PEOPLE LEARN THE MOST THROUGH FAILURE
3. Thinking Errors — 27
4. Failing Fast and Cheap — 41

II. PEOPLE FAIL THE MOST PLAYING GAMES
5. Die Trying — 55
6. Obstacles and Magic Circles — 69

III. THEREFORE, GAMES ARE THE BEST WAY FOR PEOPLE TO LEARN
7. The First Step to Gamifying — 85
8. The "Fail to Learn" Gamification Model — 105

CONCLUSION
9. The Playing Human — 121

Thank You — 125
Acknowledgments — 127
About the Author — 131
Notes — 133

OUR MANIFESTO

1. People learn the most through failure.
2. People fail the most playing games.
3. Therefore, **games** are the best way for people to learn.

INTRODUCTION

1

WELCOME TO THE REVOLUTION

THE YEAR IS 300,000 B.C., and you are one hungry caveman.

There's a problem though. You're not a skilled enough hunter to just wander out and bag a saber-toothed tiger.

Your stomach growls.

You consider your options:

1. Just start hunting. Stalk those tigers day and night. Sure, you'll be putting yourself at risk, what with the lack of sleep and shelter. And all it takes is one slip-up for you to become cat food. On the plus side, the real world is the best place to quickly develop your skills.

2. Stay at home. Hunting is incredibly dangerous, so you should really only do it when absolutely necessary. Skill-building is not worth dying for. Who cares if you end up less interested and less motivated to hunt? Once you get desperate enough, those survival skills will come to you. Probably.

Neither of these sound ideal, so let's see what's behind Door #3. (Did cavemen even have doors?) Anyway, there's one final option that's an alternative to constant hunting or constant hiding:

3. Build yourself a target that *looks* like a saber-toothed tiger. Practice stalking and throwing your spears at that instead. Unlike Option 1, if you miss, you won't be eaten. In fact, you might build skills even faster because you'll be able to practice over and over without having to waste time fleeing real-life predators. And unlike Option 2, your target-practice game will do more than keep you safe. As you play, you will also be motivated to find better and better ways to win.

Congratulations. You've just invented the core elements of a learning game. And while we may have stopped hunting prehistoric cats, we *still* take similar approaches to building modern-day skills.

FAIL TO LEARN

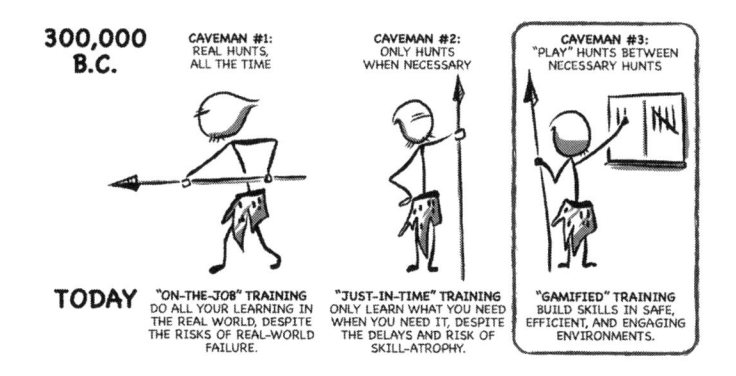

300,000 B.C.

CAVEMAN #1: REAL HUNTS, ALL THE TIME

CAVEMAN #2: ONLY HUNTS WHEN NECESSARY

CAVEMAN #3: "PLAY" HUNTS BETWEEN NECESSARY HUNTS

TODAY

"ON-THE-JOB" TRAINING DO ALL YOUR LEARNING IN THE REAL WORLD, DESPITE THE RISKS OF REAL-WORLD FAILURE.

"JUST-IN-TIME" TRAINING ONLY LEARN WHAT YOU NEED WHEN YOU NEED IT, DESPITE THE DELAYS AND RISK OF SKILL-ATROPHY.

"GAMIFIED" TRAINING BUILD SKILLS IN SAFE, EFFICIENT, AND ENGAGING ENVIRONMENTS.

Welcome to the gamified training revolution. It's been 300,000 years in the making.

Today, "gamification" is one of the hottest trends in the learning and development industry. Its $9 billion market in 2020 is projected to grow to over $30 billion in the next five years.[1] Half of today's startup companies are integrating gamification into their strategies, and corporate organizations are buying gamified products at an exponential rate.[2]

But there are a few problems with this hot new trend.

1. Up to 80% of gamified solutions won't meet their business objectives[3]

2. When people "gamify" something, they often make it too complex and confusing[4]

Oh, and also this...

3. Most people aren't even sure what "gamification" means.

This is a short book because it's meant to cut through the clutter. We'll get right to the core of "gamification," and we'll do this by focusing on two essential elements that are often overlooked: how we create the boundaries to *play* within games, and how we deal with *failure* in games.

But let's start by agreeing on what the word "gamification" means.

A "DELIBERATELY UGLY" WORD

> *[T]his was the point when I coined the deliberately ugly word "gamification," by which I meant applying game-like accelerated user interface design to make electronic transactions both enjoyable and fast.[5]*
>
> NICK PELLING

So what is "gamification," I mean, besides a clunky and "deliberately ugly" word?

Even though this official term has only been around for a handful of years, the practices behind gamification extend back throughout human history—and that's not even counting any tiger-hunting, game-playing ancestors. If someone ever tells you that gamification is just the latest fad, here are a few facts you can politely throw in their face...

- When the first auction house opened in Sweden in 1674, using motivators like competition, chance, and bidding to get people involved...that was "gamification."

- When 18th-century businesses started giving customers copper tokens with every purchase, explaining that the tokens could be redeemed for future prizes...that was "gamifying" the retail market.

- When loyalty programs exploded throughout the 19th and 20th centuries (everything from hotel points to shopper perks to frequent flier miles)...they were all using game-based tools.

- When the Boy Scouts was founded in 1908, and began awarding badges to its members for various accomplishments...that was "gamification," too.

- And of course, as businesses continue to adopt new ways to motivate and incentivize employees (through recognition programs,

team competitions, product narratives, etc.),
they are all "gamifying" the workplace.[6]

These are just a few examples of what gamification has looked like throughout our history. To tie them all together, here's a straightforward definition from a true thought leader in the industry.

> *Gamification is using game-based mechanics, aesthetics and game thinking to engage people, motivate action, promote learning, and solve problems.*[7]

KARL KAPP

If we've successfully used gamification through nearly all of human history, then why do 80% of business gamification solutions fail? Why aren't we better at using this fundamental strategy in the training, education, and corporate worlds?

There's a lot we can blame actually, from the rise of behaviorist thinking in the 20th century to the corporate overreliance on extrinsic motivators. This book will unpack how these barriers were formed, and show you a way to guide your learners past them. The strategies discussed here will work for nearly any environment, whether you're working with adult learners or within an elementary school. No matter where you are, there's a benefit to embracing the practices of failure and play, two key tools in the next learning revolution.

WHY WRITE THIS BOOK

On the first day of third grade, my teacher explained that, in addition to the math and spelling we would have to do on the board (in front of everyone!), we also would no longer get an afternoon recess because we were "serious students" now.

I should have revolted then and there.

I should have called her out for totally missing the point of social learning and play theory. But even if my eight-year-old self had known about these concepts, I probably wouldn't have argued. I wasn't much of a revolutionary back then.

So instead of speaking up about the flawed nature of public embarrassment and reduced playtime, I deployed a different strategy. I faked being sick. Every morning, I'd moan and clutch my stomach until my mom let me stay home.

I missed weeks of school because I didn't know how to feel about failing and playing in the world.

I'm calling this a "manifesto" because I'm finally speaking up for that confused little third-grader. I'm also speaking up for learning and development professionals who think our educational system has the wrong ideas about failure and play. Both failure and play bring something essential to a learning experience, and both are sorely lacking in how we teach people today.

I also think there's a bit of failure and playfulness at the heart of the manifesto genre. Manifestos are audacious, actionable, and unafraid to push new ideas right up to the bleeding edge of their industry. That's what I hope to do in this brief book. If you don't agree with some of the points I make here, then I'm probably doing something right.

WAIT, WHY CALL IT A "MANIFESTO"?

THAT WAY, IT'S STILL EDGY AND COOL IF NO ONE READS IT.

Manifestos also have numbered lists. Don't ask me why—maybe amidst all that edginess and action, revolutionaries forget their talking points. So here are my enumerated claims, which you'll see combine to form a syllogism (*If A = B and B = C, then C = A*).

1. People learn the most through failure.
2. People fail the most playing games.
3. Therefore, **games** are the best way for people to learn.

Each part of this book will explore a different section of this argument. We'll see how modern society has muddled the concepts of failure and play, from the behaviorists of World War II to the more recent (and misguided) crusade against video games. I'll show you how new research is uncovering the true value of error-based and game-based learning. And we'll end with some actionable tips and strategies you can use to start gamifying your own learning environments.

I believe one of the reasons that "gamification" is so popular right now is that people are starting to question these outdated perspectives on failure and play. I wrote this book so you'll feel prepared to lead these conversations. Whether you're discussing the best way to build skills in software development or Paleolithic hunting, understanding the elements of failure and play will give you the tools you need to spark your own revolution.

POP QUIZ

Nothing jump-starts our body's threat-response system quite like the phrase "Pop Quiz." If you're one of the many who feel some level of test anxiety, your brain might be readying its primitive "fight or flight" response. But at the same time, it's also rallying the more advanced cortical structures needed for complex reasoning. This is a unique pairing, and one I want to shamelessly exploit throughout this book to give you some key facts and figures.

Don't worry, no one is grading your performance. Or if you're masochistic enough to grade yourself, just know that *failing* can sometimes be a better way to remember this information (as you'll soon see). We'll start with some questions about the professional training industry, just to check in on the current state of things. Good luck!

WHAT PERCENTAGE OF A LEARNER'S TRAINING DO THEY ACTUALLY USE ON THE JOB?

    a) As little as 10%
    b) About 50%
    c) About 70%
    d) As much as 90%

Answer: **A.** Some studies[8] show that only 10-40% of training is actually used on the job. That's low, even accounting for all those filler slides you see in presentations (cat GIFs, blurry cartoons screenshot straight from the internet, etc., etc.).

WHAT PERCENTAGE OF TRAINING DO INSTRUCTIONAL DESIGNERS BELIEVE EFFECTIVELY MEETS LEARNER'S NEEDS?

    a) Under 20%
    b) Under 40%
    c) Over 60%
    d) Over 80%

Answer: **B.** In a survey of over one thousand Instructional Designers, these professionals believed they only effectively met 38% of their learner needs.[9] So not only is a majority of training not used on the job, but even instructional designers themselves don't believe their trainings are effective.

HOW MANY TIMES SHOULD A LEARNER FAIL BEFORE THEY SUCCESSFULLY MASTER A CONCEPT OR SKILL?

a) Zero. In a perfect world, learners would perform flawlessly.

b) Seriously, it's zero. Why struggle if you don't have to?

c) Zero! Enough already.

d) Fine, a million. A million fails for each success. Happy now?

Answer: It might be less than a million, but it's definitely more than zero. Want to learn more about the real-world ratios of failure and play? Read on.

CHAPTER SUMMARY

- Humans have always combined play and failure to create learning environments. But educational and behavioral movements over the last century have caused us to forget just how effective these two basic concepts are.

- "Gamification" refers to the application of game mechanics (e.g. points, characters, competition, etc.) and game thinking to engage people, motivate action, promote learning, and solve problems.

- Gamification is a hot topic right now, especially in the corporate training world. But it's also getting confusing, and cluttered. This book will help you break down gamification into its two core elements (failure and play), and show you how they will be key tools in the next learning revolution.

2

HOW MUCH DO YOU FAIL AND PLAY?

LET'S skip forward a few hundred thousand years, where we as a species went from hunting saber-toothed tigers in the jungle to hunting dust bunnies under the refrigerator.

In the 1980s, entrepreneur James Dyson wanted to create a new way for people to clean. Dyson was trying to invent a new kind of vacuum, one that didn't require a cumbersome and inefficient waste bag. After a lot of thinking, he built his first prototype.

It failed.

Undeterred, Dyson went back to the drawing board and built out another prototype.

That one didn't work either. Neither did the one after that. Neither did the next hundred versions.

Dyson wasn't afraid to see this growing line of failed experiments. It's a good thing, too, because the line of rejects didn't stop at a hundred prototypes. Not even close. Before he successfully created his revolutionary bagless vacuum cleaner, James Dyson went through 5,126 failed iterations.[1]

TEST #3,857

"You never learn from success," Dyson later said, "but you do learn from failure. We have to embrace failure and almost get a kick out of it...Life is a mountain of solvable problems and I enjoy that."[2]

Dyson probably did not expect to fail over five thousand times. But his playful willingness to "get a kick out of it," allowed him to remain open to a solution. And Dyson is certainly not the only one who took a playful approach to innovation. In his book *Wonderland: How Play Made the Modern World*, Steven Johnson reveals that many cornerstones of the modern world, from probability theory to artificial intelligence, came from people just kicking back and playing around.[3]

And yet, we continue to falsely believe that success should be serious work, and that failure should be a shameful thing you relegate to back rooms and trash bins.

Well, this chapter is here to give you a harsh reality check. Like Dyson said, I hope you get a kick out of it.

THE MYTHS OF SERIOUSNESS AND SUCCESS

For many years, we've collectively encouraged the myth that successful people fail and play as little as possible. We might grant an inventor a few botched prototypes, or allow Einstein to stick out his tongue on occasion, but we certainly don't consider these acts to have value themselves.

How wrong we are.

Wait...just *how* wrong are we?

How often should we actually expect to fail? How much of our time should we devote to unstructured play? Before we go any further in our exploration of gamified learning, I challenge you to do some self-reflection on how much failure and play you let into your own life.

This is especially important for learning and development professionals to think about. How much failure and play you allow yourself reflects in how much failure and play you provide your learners. We can't teach people effectively when we're still buying into the myth of flawless, serious success.

Perhaps the best way to bust this myth is to look at the data. The rest of this chapter will give you some failure and play ratios to consider as we set out on this training revolution. These numbers are based on studies and interviews conducted by people in both the academic and corporate sectors. My guess is that—like me—you are still seriously underestimating how many mistakes and playful moments you should be living with.

Because it turns out James Dyson's five thousand failures might be on the shallow end of the pool.

THE PLAY RATIO: ONE IN EIGHT

In his book *Play*, Dr. Stuart Brown explains that adults are "pushed from play, shamed into rejecting it by a culture that doesn't understand the human need for it and doesn't respect it."[4]

We educators and trainers have certainly done a lot to reinforce this, especially those of us working with adult learners. "The message," Brown continues, "is that if you are a serious person doing serious work, you should be serious."

What's sad is that, in addition to depriving our learners of fun, joyful experiences, we might actually be creating less effective ways to learn and remember things. According to Judy Willis in *The Neuroscience of Joyful Education*, "when we scrub joy and comfort from the classroom, we distance our students from effective information processing and long-term memory storage."[5]

So we should encourage people to play more. But *how much more?*

Dr. Jane McGonigal has spent years studying and speaking on the positive effects of play, with a special emphasis on video games. She's collected research from all over, including how games like *Tetris* can help people recover from PTSD, or how virtual worlds can be even more effective than morphine for relieving pain.[6]

What makes McGonigal's play research so much more impressive is the fact that she's studying one of the most heavily critiqued mediums. Video games have been blamed (usually falsely) for everything from increased aggression to decreased sleep. Perhaps as a way to dispute some of these misconceptions, McGonigal provides a startling data point for us to measure out how much we should play.

To start, McGonigal cites a 2012 meta-analysis of 38 randomized controlled trials that showed "significant promise for video games to improve psychological health outcomes."[7] Thanks to this meta-analysis (and others) we have plenty of data to support the claim that video games *can* offer health benefits. But how often should we actually be playing them?

To answer this, McGonigal spent five years tracking gameplay in all kinds of people, from those casually gaming on the couch to those serving in the military. When she compared the collected survey data, she did indeed find a magic number for playing games:

> *Twenty-one hours a week is the tipping point. People who play video games three or fewer hours per day tend to reap the benefits of play.*[8]

For most of us, three hours a day probably seems

pretty high. Even hard-core gamers might agree. In their *State of Online Gaming* report, Limelight Networks said the average gamer spends just over seven hours *a week* playing.[9] And while this is up nearly 20% from last year, it's still well under McGonigal's twenty-one-hour-per-week threshold.

That means most of us, including the "average gamer" could at least triple the ratio of games in our life and still see benefits.

If twenty-one hours of play per week is the tipping point, then our overall play ratio boils down to one hour of play every eight hours.

Is your play ratio one in eight (in life or in a classroom)?

If not, how far off are you?

And what about your tolerance for failure? Because that's where the numbers start to get *really* interesting.

THE FAILURE RATIO: TEN THOUSAND TO ONE

> *I have not failed 10,000 times. I have not failed once. I have succeeded in proving that those 10,000 ways will not work.*

Thomas Edison said these now-famous words.[10] And while he probably wasn't proposing an official ratio of failure to success here, he does give us a good starting point. Surprisingly, the exact same number that Edison landed on appeared a hundred years later in an entirely different industry.

In 2011, businessman Peter Cohan started researching the success rate of startup companies. Based on the hundreds of venture capitalists and CEOs Cohan interviewed,[11] he came to this sobering realization:

> (Y)our odds of achieving start-up success on a large scale—meaning starting a company that is worth at least $1 billion—are about one in 10,000.

From Edison to Wall Street, the 10,000:1 failure ratio appears to hold true.

Now these are obviously just a couple examples of the many failure-to-success stories we could pull from. But rather than continue parsing numbers, instead ask yourself if you come even *close* to a ratio like that.

How long do you allow yourself to struggle with new material? How many times do you forgive yourself for making a mistake? How many hours do you practice something before expecting great results?

Oh, coincidentally (and somewhat contentiously[12]), do you know how long author Malcolm Gladwell believes you must practice before you achieve world-class expertise?

You guessed it: 10,000 hours.

In his book *Outliers*[13], Gladwell even dubs this the "10,000 Hour Rule." It's another example of how long we should plan to really suck at something. And it's no surprise that most of us—uncomfortable with this high rate of failure—quit early.

NUMBER OF FAILURES BEFORE ONE SUCCESS

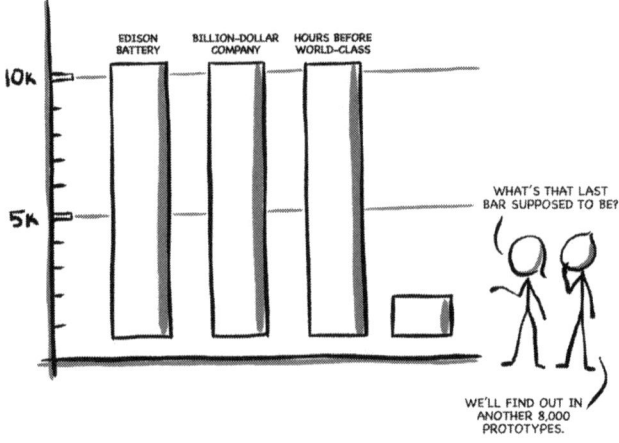

[Bar chart showing Edison Battery, Billion-Dollar Company, and Hours Before World-Class all near 10k, with a small fourth bar. Two stick figures: "WHAT'S THAT LAST BAR SUPPOSED TO BE?" "WE'LL FIND OUT IN ANOTHER 8,000 PROTOTYPES."]

WHAT'S YOUR RATIO?

A quality learning environment is built on a healthy relationship with failure and play. As learning and development professionals, we must model these relationships, and acknowledge the aversion we've come to have for both terms.

When challenging beliefs as deep-set as these (my own aversions were already in place by the third grade), it helps to fall back on objective data. I wanted to give you these suggested play and failure ratios up front because I want you to think about where your own numbers fall.

What do you consider to be an acceptable error rate? Is it different in an educational setting? What about play?

How often do you encourage free exploration in a learning environment? What about in other parts of life?

In the next two sections, we'll challenge and hopefully undo some of the misconceptions around failure and play that have somehow become standard practice in the classroom. You'll see how these misconceptions took root and, more importantly, how to weed them out.

You'll see proof that people learn the most through failure, and fail the most through games. And as the dominos start to fall, you'll see some of our deepest misconceptions about how people learn start to topple as well.

The gamified revolution is coming. Will it succeed? Yes—but it will also fail, again and again. Playfully and spectacularly.

CHAPTER SUMMARY

- In order to become good instructors and course designers, we first need to develop a healthier and more realistic expectation of the amount of failure and play that it takes to be successful.

- Even only counting video games (one of the most controversial forms of play when it comes to providing health benefits), we now know that people can play up to one out of every eight hours and still see positive benefits.

- Failure-to-success ratios can be as high as 10,000:1. A former IBM President summed it up this way. "If you want to increase your success rate, double your failure rate."[14]

I. PEOPLE LEARN THE MOST THROUGH FAILURE

3

THINKING ERRORS

THE YEAR IS 1943, and the U.S. military needs to develop an accurate, affordable way to bomb enemy targets. Who do they pick to pilot America's missiles?

Bats.

Also: Pigeons.

"Project X-Ray" was all about the bats. Its questionable reasoning went like this:

- Japanese cities have wooden structures
- Bats like to roost in wood attics
- We'll strap tiny bombs onto bats, then drop them out of planes
- They'll roost all over Japanese cities
- Then they'll explode

Project X-Ray had problems right from the start. In order to get the bats calm enough for their initial flight, the military had to freeze them, which they did by placing the bats in little ice-cube trays. Reasoning went that the bats would thaw as they fell from the plane, but reality proved this incorrect. Many of the furry popsicles never fully woke up from hibernation and died on impact.

The bats that *did* wake up sometimes chose questionable targets. Project X-Ray was eventually cancelled after several failed trials, during which the furry bombardiers managed to destroy an entire U.S. testing facility.[1]

On to the pigeons.

"Project Pigeon" was the brainchild of B.F. Skinner, who would later become one of the most well-known psychologists of the twentieth century. Skinner believed that pigeons could be taught to steer missiles using "operant conditioning." Operant conditioning is the idea that you can teach pretty much anything to anyone by simply connecting their behavior to a consequence.

B.F.'s B.F.F.

The military gave B.F. Skinner $25,000 to see if his pigeon-guided missile system fared any better than the bats did. And even though "Project Pigeon" was also eventually scrapped, Skinner *did* prove that pigeons could learn how to steer. The nose-cone of his pigeon missile still rests in the American History Museum.[2]

From this strange beginning, B.F. Skinner's theories of punishment- and reward-based learning went on to shape much of our twentieth-century education system.

Maybe the reason our education system is so backwards in its understanding of failure is because it's rooted in an eighty-year-old theory developed for birds and bombs.

THINKING INSIDE THE BOX

To get how Skinner's theory came to shape our expectations of learning, we first must know how "operant learning" works. It goes something like this:

Take a desired behavior (like pushing a lever or doing a job). Then, reinforce that behavior with one of the following:

- Add something good (*"Yum!"*)
- Add something bad (*"Ouch!"*)
- Take away something good (*"That's mine!"*)
- Take away something bad (*"Phew!"*)

Skinner proved his theory by putting animals in enclosures—now known as "Skinner Boxes." When the animal pressed a lever, a food pellet appeared (*"Yum!"*). Let the learning commence:

- Press lever → Get food
- Press lever → Get food
- Press lever → Get food

It's a beautiful system, but why stop with pigeons? Much of our education system still follows the same operant conditioning principles:

- Raise hand → Get called on
- Pass test → Get an "A"
- Press "Next" button on the screen → Get closer to the end of the boring, online compliance training

The problem with this system is that it discourages any sort of experimentation or discovery through trial-and-error. Skinner actually designed his experiments so that his pigeons would be *less likely* to make mistakes.[3] "Errors are not a function of learning," he explained.[4]

And yet, it appears his pigeons actually *did* learn better when they were allowed to fail. A recent scientific review analyzed these pigeon-studies of the mid-twentieth century and found that "the pigeon's reaction time...was faster when the learning procedure had been errorful."[5]

Even pigeons learn from their mistakes. So why aren't we changing the way we train?

It turns out, some people are. Here are some results from across the world, and with all sorts of learner groups, that show huge benefits in thinking outside the Skinner Box.

FAILING AROUND THE WORLD

In a 2017 paper, Professor Janet Metcalfe wrote that "An unwarranted reluctance to engage with errors may have held back American education."[6] Fortunately, our education system is starting to take notes from schools and studies in other countries, ones that show how valuable learning through failure can be. Here are results from just a few:

SINGAPORE

In Singapore, students were split into two groups and given math problems to solve. In the "Direct Instruction" group, students got help from their teacher every step of the way. In the "Productive Failure" group, students were left to struggle with the problems until finally discussing their failed attempts with a teacher.

Although the Productive Failure students were "ultimately unsuccessful in their problem-solving efforts,"[7] they outscored the Direct Instruction group on the final exam.[8]

JAPAN, CHINA, TAIWAN

"Learning about what is wrong may hasten understanding of why the correct procedures are appropriate," write Harold Stevenson and James Stigler in their book *The Learning Gap*.[9] These social scientists studied classrooms across the U.S., Japan, China, and Taiwan.

Among other things, they found that, while American teachers ignored errors and only praised correct answers, Japanese teachers instead explored common mistakes, and encouraged students to try out both right and wrong solutions, and figure out how they got to each.[10] Stevenson and Stigler found that, since errors are often interpreted as failures, American teachers "strive to avoid situations where this might happen."

This might explain why the U.S. has fallen so far behind in educational rankings. The Trends in International Mathematics and Science Study (TIMSS) showed that children in East Asian countries (including Singapore and Japan, two of the countries cited here) have dominated the charts for the past twenty years.[11]

UNITED STATES

We'll end with a ray of hope for American educators and trainers. In a recent study from UCLA, researchers gave one group of students a traditional classroom approach to solving math problems: lecture, followed by examples and homework. The second group was simply given problems to solve: no explanation, no answers.

Even worse, these problems were purposefully written to be confusing.

WHAT IS THE AIRSPEED VELOCITY OF AN UNLADEN SWALLOW?

Poor Group 2 tried and failed until right before the final exam, when they were given a quick explanation of the key concepts. It might sound like a barbaric way to teach, but Group 2 actually scored 10% higher on the exam than the traditional instruction group. And the learning didn't stop there.

Both groups were then given a brand new math topic (one that nobody had seen before). Half the students in Group 2 passed the new test, compared to only 21 percent of the traditional instruction group.[12]

METCALFE IS RIGHT. AMERICAN EDUCATORS' reluctance to engage with errors is certainly unwarranted. But fortunately, many have learned to overcome this reluctance. And thanks to new brain-mapping technologies, we now have neurological proof of how we learn when we fail.

POP QUIZ

How about we ground the next section on neuroscience with an experiential activity? Try to answer each of these brain teaser and general knowledge questions (no cheating). After you answer each one, rank on a scale of 1-10 how confident you are that you got the question right.

WHAT IS THE NEXT NUMBER IN THIS SEQUENCE?

1, 4, 5, 6, 7, 9, 11

Confidence: __

YOU ARE IN A ROOM WITH NO METAL OBJECTS EXCEPT FOR TWO IDENTICAL IRON BARS. ONE BAR IS A MAGNET, THE OTHER IS NOT MAGNETIZED. HOW CAN YOU TELL WHICH IS WHICH?

Confidence: __

HOW MANY BONES ARE IN THE TYPICAL ADULT HUMAN BODY?

Confidence: __

PLACE THESE EVENTS OF HUMAN HISTORY IN CHRONOLOGICAL ORDER:

__ The rise and fall of the Aztec Empire
__ The invention of algebra
__ The initial building of the Great Wall
__ The Harlem Renaissance
__ Newton's theory of gravity

Confidence: __

THIS IS YOUR BRAIN ON FAILURE

I definitely would have failed that quiz. And then I probably would have grumbled to myself something along the lines of:

"No one would have guessed that."

"That question was poorly written."

"Trivia knowledge like this has absolutely zero value in the real world."

And while my internal monologue would have been working overtime to soothe my ego (more on this in a later chapter), something entirely different would have been going on inside my brain.

Whether or not I thought the test was fair, whether or

not I got the questions wrong, my brain will keep on learning.

In fact, getting the answers wrong may even help my brain learn *better*.

"It may be worthwhile to allow and even encourage students to commit and correct errors while they are in low-stakes learning situations rather than to assiduously avoid errors at all costs," writes Metcalfe.[13] Other researchers have arrived at similar conclusions. A Michigan State neurological study found that people who had a "growth mindset" (i.e., believing that failure is an opportunity to grow) had a larger neurological response when they made a mistake. These growth-mindset mistake-makers were more likely to do better in future performances.[14]

So our brains experience a natural boost in neurological activity when we make a mistake. But—even weirder—they can also get *physically bigger*.

According to a report from *Scientific American*, your brain actually grows like some mad-scientist experiment during learning scenarios. And, as Forbes columnist Simon Casuto writes, "while the brain returns to close to its original size after the learning experience, it retains new neural pathways by taking in new information, compiling the key takeaways from trial and error."[15]

So there you have it: Neurological proof that we learn from failure. Our brains can increase their size and improve their neural pathways, especially when we can see where we've made the error, and compare it to the correct answer.

Which reminds me: Here are the correct answers to the previous quiz:

POP QUIZ - ANSWERS

WHAT IS THE NEXT NUMBER IN THIS SEQUENCE?

1, 4, 5, 6, 7, 9, 11...

Answer: 100. It's the next number that, when spelled out, doesn't contain the letter "t." You probably could also come up with several correct answers that actually involve math, but you're dealing with an English major here...sorry.[16]

YOU ARE IN A ROOM WITH NO METAL OBJECTS EXCEPT FOR TWO IDENTICAL IRON BARS. ONE BAR IS A MAGNET, THE OTHER IS NOT MAGNETIZED. HOW CAN YOU TELL WHICH IS WHICH?

Answer: Either hang the bars on a string and see which one turns to the north (like a compass needle would). Or, hold one bar and touch its end to the middle of the second bar. If the bars get closer, you're holding the magnetized one.[17]

HOW MANY BONES ARE IN THE TYPICAL ADULT HUMAN BODY?

Answer: 206. However, even the answer to this basic biology question isn't so black-and-white. This number doesn't count the tiny bones in your ears, or people who have extra rib bones, or bones that may have fused irregularly. And when we're babies, we start with closer to 270 bones, several of which gradually grow together. So your answer might be very unique to your own body.

PLACE THESE EVENTS OF HUMAN HISTORY IN CHRONOLOGICAL ORDER:

1. The initial building of the Great Wall (circa 220 B.C.)
2. The invention of algebra (circa 820)
3. The rise and fall of the Aztec Empire (circa 1150-1521)
4. Newton's theory of gravity (1687)
5. The Harlem Renaissance (1918 - mid-1930s)

Remember, no matter how much your internal monologue is yelling at me over the fairness of these questions (*"You never said there was string in the room with the iron bars!"*), your brain is already building new neural networks, in case it ever needs to reference these bits of obscure trivia in the future.

And the more questions you got wrong, the harder at work your brain might be.

CONFIDENTLY WRONG

One final note on the brain and failure: Remember those confidence ratings you placed by your initial quiz answers? It turns out this is another easy way we can teach ourselves to learn from mistakes.

Multiple studies show that the more confident we are in a *wrong* answer, the more likely we'll be to remember the right answer once we learn it.[18] Metcalfe found these same results in her *Learning from Errors* research. In the past, researchers believed that if you were highly confident in your error, it would be that much harder to learn the right answer.

But in fact the opposite is true.[19] When we're highly confident in our answer, and that answer turns out to be wrong, not only is the brain quick to overwrite and correct the info, but we're also *more likely* to remember and learn from that mistake.

The educators and trainers out there should recognize this as a quick instructional design hack: What if you added a "confidence rating" column to your next test? It costs no extra grading time, and research supports the added benefits it brings.

Now all you have to do is soothe your failure-averse, operant-conditioned learners, and tell them that it's okay to get things wrong from time to time. Remind them that our brains are resilient and ever-expanding.

After all, we're not pigeons.

CHAPTER SUMMARY

- The popularity of behaviorism and operant conditioning in the twentieth century had a huge influence on teaching methods. It also helped instill (at least in the U.S.) a deep aversion to trial-and-error learning.

- We're finally starting to collect proof that people learn better when they're allowed to struggle and fail. We've measured this by doing everything from comparing classrooms around the world to mapping the inner workings of the brain.

- Trainers and teachers can quickly incorporate failure-based learning into courses by including things like confidence ratings on tests, which can trigger the brain to learn more from its mistakes.

4

FAILING FAST AND CHEAP

A FLEDGLING COMPANY WAS STRUGGLING. Their CEO, a man named Frederick Smith, was trying to revolutionize the package delivery industry by utilizing planes rather than trucks to courier goods. Smith had collected over $80 million in investments, loans, and inheritance to make his vision a reality. But after a rough first few years, and the rising fuel costs of the early 1970s, Smith now faced bankruptcy.

And he prepared himself to say goodbye to his new little company...FedEx.

FedEx was down to its final $5,000 when Smith decided to take action. So with that last five grand, Smith did what any CEO would do.

He went to Vegas.

That's right. Fred Smith took the last bit of cash from a company that was millions of dollars in debt and he went to the blackjack tables for the weekend.

By Monday, he'd won $27,000.

It was enough to keep FedEx afloat, and enough to get them to where they are today, a corporate giant worth billions.

Roger Frock, a former Senior Vice President of FedEx, wrote about this baffling turn of events in his book *Changing How the World Does Business*. Frock describes confronting Smith, and asking how he could have done such a thing with the company's last few dollars. What did Smith say in response?

"What difference does it make? Without the funds for the fuel companies, we couldn't have flown anyway."[1]

LOSS AVERSION

If you had been in Smith's position, would you have done the same thing?

For most of us, the answer is no. Even just reading about Smith's story, imagining the millions of dollars of debt and picturing that final, paltry stack of $5,000, most of us don't think about how we could grow that money. Instead, we think about how to avoid losing any more.

This desire to avoid further losses is buried deep in our psyche. Cognitive psychologists have a term for this basic human behavior. They call it "loss aversion," and it dictates how people approach everything from gambling to foreign policy to education.[2]

Imagine someone approached you with this proposition: They'll flip a coin, and if it's heads, you pay them $100. But if it's tails, they'll pay you $100.

Most people refuse to take this wager, even though

they have just as much of a chance to win as they do to lose. The theory of loss aversion explains why.

According to psychologists Daniel Kahneman and Amos Tversky, we typically have to see *twice* as much of a payout before we're willing to risk anything.[3] People won't take the $100 coin-flip bet unless they could stand to win $200.

Tversky found this two-to-one loss aversion ratio holds true whether we're wagering $10 or $10,000. No matter the joy we get from winning, we'll always feel twice as much pain if we lose.

How does this apply to learning from failure? As Jon Wergin writes in his book *Deep Learning in a Disorienting World*, "loss aversion is one of the most dangerous cognitive traps." Wergin explains that when we're motivated by fear of loss, we're operating in a "fixed mindset," that belief that we cannot change our surroundings or our qualities. You'll remember from the previous chapter that the opposite of a fixed mindset—a growth mindset—is what leads to all those neurological benefits from failure.

"We need to overcome loss aversion," Wergin continues, "and be willing to take on reasonable risks."[4]

Many successful CEOs have found a way to do this, and their behavior may have more to do with Vegas than you think.

WHAT GAMBLING, ALCOHOL, AND BUSINESS HAVE IN COMMON

Scientists are starting to isolate the chemicals in our brains that create our emotional reaction to failure and loss. One of the responsible chemicals is a neurotransmitter called norepinephrine. The majority of us, having an average amount of norepinephrine, will categorically fear failure and avoid loss.

However, some people have uniquely high levels of norepinephrine in certain parts of their brain. And studies show that these people are *less* affected when they lose.[5] Who are these people? Perhaps unsurprisingly, it's those addicted to gambling and drinking.

But it's also high-powered executives.

A study published in *Nature* found that both pathological gamblers and those with alcohol dependence have a reduced sense of loss aversion.[6] Other research has found that these same traits show up more often in CEOs.[7] Novelty-seeking and risk-taking behavior can be great for a corporate leader, but this same loss-averse approach can also correlate with addiction.

Obviously, most business owners do not struggle with gambling or alcohol dependence. Yet it's interesting to consider where and why this overlap in risk-taking behavior exists. It might explain some of the reasons why Smith chose to save his company by going to the blackjack tables.

When faced with a high-risk choice, a growth-minded CEO thinks differently than the rest of us. They are more likely to take a calculated leap of faith. They can analyze the odds without as much of a loss-aversion haze. And armed with this perspective, they can ask the same question Smith did, the one that terrifies the rest of us when we're down to our last dollar.

"What difference does it make?"

THE SECRET FORMULA

Besides potentially having a different balance of brain chemicals, there's another trick up the sleeve of many successful and high-powered individuals. Many of them share the same secret formula when it comes to failure. And more than any neurotransmitter, knowledge of this secret formula can help you become more successful, too.

Okay, so this formula is not so secret. In fact, lots of

leaders and influencers, from CEOs to scientists, shout it out from the rooftops.[8]

> *Fail fast, fail hard, fail often.*
>
> RESHMA SAUJANI, FOUNDER OF GIRLS WHO CODE

> *To develop working ideas efficiently, I try to fail as fast as I can.*
>
> RICHARD FEYMAN, NOBEL PRIZE WINNING PHYSICIST

> *If you are not embarrassed by the first version of your product, you've launched too late.*
>
> REID HOFFMAN, CO-FOUNDER AND EXECUTIVE CHAIRMAN OF LINKEDIN

What makes the world's innovators so successful is their ability to fail *quickly* and *inexpensively*. And this "fail fast and cheap" formula is what we desperately need in the learning and development world today.

Sadly, traditional methods of education sometimes seem to apply the exact *opposite* formula:

- **Instead of failing fast**...we make learners wait until a final exam to check their knowledge. Sometimes we delay test results by weeks or even months.

- **Instead of failing cheap**...we make learners repeat large portions of work or even retake entire courses when they get enough wrong.

Could a "fail fast and cheap" formula actually work in a learning environment? Actually, it already has.

FAIL FAST, LEARN FAST

James Pennebaker and Samuel Gosling are professors at the University of Texas at Austin. They ran an experiment with over 900 students in a psychology class, in which students were given *daily* quizzes on content. Students also got *immediate* feedback on any quiz questions they got wrong. In other words, they were allowed to fail quickly (every day) and cheaply (immediate feedback that didn't destroy their final grade).

The overall grades of these students were then measured against previous classes, who had taken the same course in a traditional college format (think infrequent, "high cost" exams). Not only did the daily-quiz students average *half a letter grade higher*, but they also performed better in *other* courses they took during that same semester.[9]

This approach works with adult learners, too. In the 1980s, a cognitive scientist named Philip Kellman was studying to become a pilot. Kellman realized that much of his education had to do with perceptual learning, specifically, the ability to spot patterns and information hidden in all of those cockpit instruments and readouts.

Kellman wanted to create a quicker way for students to get an instinctive "feel" for the complex instrument panel of a plane. He developed what he called a "perceptual learning model," or PLM.

The core function of a PLM is to *quickly* present information—in Kellman's case, different combinations of cockpit readouts—with a multiple-choice option for what that information meant. In Kellman's PLM, if a learner answered wrong, there was an incorrect sound, followed immediately by the next question. In other words, the feedback is not only quick, but also, in a sense, cheap. There was no punishment for guessing incorrectly.

Kellman tested his PLM with a group of both novice and expert pilots. After only an hour, the novice pilots could read the panels as well as pilots who had 1,000 hours of flight time. As writer Benedict Carey describes in *How We Learn*, even though Kellman's model was "a videogame, basically," he had managed to build "the same reading skill, at least on ground, *in 1/1,000th of the time.*"[10]

How did this happen? Applying what we know about our brain's responses to failure, it's no surprise that each error helps the brain forge new neural pathways. Kellman's learners were quickly and subconsciously absorbing information that took others years to learn.

Perceptual Learning Models have been used in other

industries as well. One PLM study measured how effectively medical students could learn a specific surgical technique. Students in the experiment scored *four times higher* than their equally experienced peers, after just *thirty minutes* of a PLM practice session.[11]

Writer Benedict Carey wasn't disparaging Kellman when he called his PLM a "videogame." In fact, Carey himself had been wanting to use PLMs to educate himself on a very specific topic.

After being embarrassed at a museum for his lack of art knowledge, Carey had his daughter mock up an Art History PLM for him. She took 120 paintings from different historic movements (Expressionism, Dadaism, Romanticism, etc.), and paired each image with a choice of twelve styles. "If I chose right, a bell rang and the check symbol flashed on the screen," Carey explains. "If I guessed wrong, a black 'X' appeared and the correct answer was highlighted."

NAME THE ABSTRACT EXPRESSIONIST AND THEIR MEDIUM

A) POLLAK, ALKYD ENAMELS

B) 2-YEAR-OLD, BANANA PUREE

C) ROTHKO, OIL AND ACRYLIC

D) FLY, WINDSHIELD

After practicing in this ad hoc PLM, Carey took a final test, in which he saw *new* paintings from those artistic styles (not the same paintings he practiced with, to be sure Carey had indeed learned how to distinguish between artistic periods, and not just recognize specific paintings).

And the results? "Thirty out of thirty-six correct, 80 percent," Carey reported. "Not bad for an hour's work."[12]

HOW "FAST AND CHEAP" IS YOUR AUDIENCE LEARNING?

How many quizzes and tests were in the last course you designed, taught, or attended?

How far apart were they spaced?

How long did learners have to wait before they got feedback?

What was the punishment, or "cost," of failing these tests?

We've been using a backwards ratio in the training and education industry. Too many courses combine a low failure rate and a high failure cost. As more and more studies show, we need to turn this on its head.

- ***Increase*** your failure rate.
- ***Decrease*** your failure cost.

We need to get over our fear of failure and think outside the Skinner boxes of the 20th century. The more we encourage learners to try and fail, the better, faster, and stronger their learning will be.

In the next section, we'll look at a sector that's incredibly successful at getting people to embrace their failures. Grab your chess board and your extra lives, because we're entering the world of games.

CHAPTER SUMMARY

- Most humans experience something called "loss aversion," to the extent that they feel *twice* as much pain from losing as they do joy from winning. One way to address this in learning environments is to lower the stakes of those losses, which can encourage more risk-taking behavior.

- A not-so-secret formula of success is to "fail fast and cheap." You can apply this same strategy to a course or curriculum. Design your material so that learners can fail without losing too much of their time or grade.

- Techniques like the one used by Perceptual Learning Models (PLMs) are proving how a "fail fast and cheap" approach to learning can be successful across many professional education settings.

II. PEOPLE FAIL THE MOST PLAYING GAMES

5

DIE TRYING

"PRESS the green button to pick up the gun."

"No, the green button."

"*Green* button."

I had never played a first-person shooter before. In fact, it was quickly becoming clear that I'd barely picked up a video game controller. My younger brother Collin, on the other hand, was a gaming pro. So I sat and listened carefully to his patient instructions over the phone. We were about to head into battle, and it was his job to help me survive.

But I was still the older brother, and I hated looking dumb in front of Collin. So I insisted the first game we play be something he'd never tried before either.

The game started, and our avatars were suddenly in the virtual wilds of Northwestern America. It was a fitting location since the two of us were separated by the *actual* wilds of Northwestern America. Say what you will about technology, but it's certainly made online cooperative gaming a breeze.

Yet, despite this high-tech platform, I still couldn't figure out how to make my avatar pick up his stupid gun.

"Someone's coming." Collin's voice came through my earpiece, as I caught the blur of movement on my screen.

I gave up on the gun and steered my avatar behind a large crate. I'd seen the previews for this game. I knew it was going to get bloody.

"Are they out there?" I realized a second too late that I was whispering into my headset, as if the bots in the game could hear me.

"Dunno. Hang on a minute."

I watched Collin's character glide past me. He conjured up a ridiculously large rifle out of thin air, then he ducked out the door.

BANG!

"Yup," Collin said, unfazed after experiencing what I could only imagine was a quick and gruesome death. "There's an ambush waiting for us out front."

I froze, both onscreen and in real life. This game actually pumped in heartbeat sounds over the audio track. As if it wasn't enough to feel my own heart in my throat.

All of a sudden, I saw Collin run past me again.

"Wait, I thought you just died," I said.

"Instant respawn, man. Hang on a minute."

He poked his head out the door again.

BANG!

"Dang it. Okay, going left might not be an option."

I thought I saw a bullet flash above my crate. I tried to make my avatar crouch down even lower. Meanwhile, Collin breezed by me for a third time.

BANG!

"Yeah. Definitely don't go left."

"How many lives do we get?"

"Lives? Infinite." Collin said, as if confused by the question. He raced by me once more. He was moving faster this time, already getting familiar with the game's controls.

"What should I do?" I asked, spinning my crouched character in a desperate circle.

BANG!

"Come join me this time. No? Well then I'll just—"

BANG!

"Oh, I see what they're doing now. Maybe we should try—"

BANG!

I risked a glance over the top of my crate. Collin was already out front for a seventh time, guns blazing. His avatar looked close to death (again), but he also looked like he'd gotten even farther away from our starting point.

BANG!

This time a bullet hit *me*. My screen flashed. "Am I dead?" I shouted. "Where are you going? You're supposed to help me survive!"

By the time I finally poked my head out the door, all the bad guys were gone and Collin's character was waving to me from the top of the hill.

"Here's a survival tip," he said. "Try dying."

DEATH AND PERMADEATH

In 2014, the "Golden Joystick" award for Best Game of the Year went to an action role-player called *Dark Souls II*. In addition to the sweeping journey *Dark Souls II* took players on, it also gave some great behind-the-scenes data. We got to see how often players of *Dark Souls II* died.

Adding up just the *Dark Souls* console gamers (e.g., people who played on PlayStation, Xbox, etc.), people were dying in this game a whopping 150,443 times per hour, which equates to 42 *deaths every second*.

That means, in 2014, the death rate in *Dark Souls II* was 23 times higher than the actual death rate in the real world.

In order to beat *Dark Souls II* on PlayStation 3, a player died 860 times on average.[1] That's not quite a Thomas Edison level, but a failure-to-success ratio of 860:1 is still larger than most of us would be comfortable with.

Seeing these numbers in print makes me wonder why I hid behind that stupid crate for so long.

I'd say I have a healthy fear of death. It keeps me from base-jumping and lion-taming, but it also apparently keeps me from developing any skills as a game-player.

Death is one of the most common learning mechanisms in games. From the classic chess board to the zombie hordes of *Resident Evil*, games help us learn by killing us over and over again. Your average gamer expects to die in nearly everything they play. To them, death and rebirth is just a dressed-up version of trial and error.

It's usually only the very experienced gamers who seek challenges without a "respawn" option. In these rare environments, if you die, you're done. No do-overs. No refresh from the last save-point. In the gaming world, it's known as "permadeath."

Even for experienced video gamers "permadeath" can be an agonizing thing to experience. Just ask Phil Watson, who holds the world record for longest survival time in "Hardcore" mode of the video game *Minecraft*. This mode combines all of the most difficult game settings, along with a permadeath state, meaning if you die, you lose the entire world you've built.

Some of the best *Minecraft Hardcore* players are able to survive for a few weeks. Phil Watson lived in his *Minecraft* world for five years.

It made his character's demise all the more tragic. A

video of Watson's last fateful seconds (which occurred in April 2019) has over a million views online. In it, you can hear the anguished cries that lie at the heart of any permadeath scenario:

"*Noooo!! Really?! That's how I die?*"[2]

KILL THE MONKEY

When it comes to dealing with death, I'm somewhere between my little brother and Phil. To be honest, I'm probably closer to Phil, in the sense that I felt like screaming and pulling my hair every time I messed up in a game. The same applies to all the times I failed in the classroom.

Games are helping me change that perspective, and become a better learner (and facilitator) because of it.

One of the things games do to help me (and the millions of other loss-averse people out there) is to actually make failing an enjoyable, even funny experience.

Picture this: You're a monkey trapped inside a glass ball. You need to get from one side of a platform to the other. You pedal desperately through different speeds and slopes, and more often than not, you roll off the platform into the dark abyss below. You scream your high-pitched monkey scream all the way down.

This is the general premise of the game *Super Monkey Ball* 2. Like all games, you'd assume players would be most interested in beating levels and completing the game.

You'd be wrong.

Psychologists in Finland had a group of people play *Super Monkey Ball 2* while hooked up to biosensors. They wanted to see at which point in the game people experienced the biggest spikes in physiological activity.

When players achieved the set objectives of each level, their pleasure increased. When they missed an objective, their frustration increased. No surprises so far.

But then the researchers noticed something weird happening. When players deliberately tried to fail—when they purposefully sent the poor monkey spinning off into space—they registered not frustration or boredom, but pleasure. "Although the event in question represents a clear failure, several physiological indices showed that it elicited positively valenced high-arousal emotion (i.e., joy), rather than disappointment."[3]

I'll admit, there's something innately pleasurable about sending a tiny cartoon monkey screaming into the void. The researchers concluded that negative events in a game can still elicit positive emotional responses. Ultimately, they found that attaining the game's original objectives actually decreased a player's level of interest overall.[4]

Sometimes, it's just more fun to kill the monkey.

EMOTIONAL RESILIENCE

Let's face it: most of us have pretty fragile egos when it comes to learning something new. No one likes being the unskilled novice. Making a mistake doesn't often feel *good*. In fact, some of the studies that show the benefits of error-driven learning are quick to point out that it only works "if students have the *emotional resilience* to respond to mistakes adaptively and flexibly."[5]

In other words, learners have to feel secure enough and brave enough to lose. So what is the best way to create a flexible, emotional resilience to making mistakes?

Play a game.

"Despite the societal taboo against failure," one educator writes, "there is one place where it is expected and embraced – games. In particular, video games are built on the premise that progress happens through a process of experimentation, failure, and adaptation."[6]

Studies conducted by everyone from the American Psychological Association to Columbia University found the same thing.[7] Those who played games tend to be more emotionally resilient than those who do not. Some studies even found that video game players showed "significantly higher intellectual functioning, higher academic achievement, better peer relationships, and fewer mental health difficulties."[8]

A lot of this emotional resilience can be traced back to the fact that game-players can build up a bigger-picture perspective about failure. They get used to telling themselves "it's all just a game." And slowly, those fragile egos become tempered through the process of playing, until they have the steely resolve to sustain just about any error in real-life.

Games give us "a kind of lightness and freedom," educator and designer Jesper Juul explains. The reason we're okay with failing so often in games is because "we have the option of denying that *game* failure matters."[9] And the more we play, the more we can bring this perspective to other parts of our life—like a classroom or a job.

THE GAME *IS* THE ASSESSMENT

Perhaps one of the biggest reasons we build such strong resilience in games is because they trick us into taking—and passing—test after test after test. In a classroom setting, we tense up when we hear the word "exam" or "pop quiz." So games do something quite tricky instead. They make their *entire* environment into the "exam." And in doing so, they simultaneously lower the stakes while increasing the rate of learning.

Imagine if we could do the same thing in a classroom, creating a course uninterrupted by quizzes or exams, not because we stopped evaluating learning but because we found a way to make the whole course into an engaging assessment.

Dr. James Paul Gee, who has spent years studying the intersection of games and learning, points out how ridiculous a commercial game would seem if it tried to operate like a traditional classroom, and separate education from assessment:

"Think about it. If I make it through every level of *Halo*, do you really need to give me a test to see if I know everything it takes to get through every level of *Halo*?"[10]

In a game-based environment, all evaluation and

feedback happens in real-time, whether you're steering a Tetris block or shooting a basketball, "the learning is the assessment," writer Greg Toppo explains. And this entertaining—and often death-driven—assessment is one of the pleasures of playing games, "...to see instantly how well we've learned, and then to try again without fuss or interruption until we succeed."[11]

CHAPTER SUMMARY

- Games force us to confront everything from our fear of mistakes to our fear of death. But by lowering the cost of failure (e.g., instantly respawning us after we "die"), they create safe and even *joyful* ways of learning through trial and error.

- Games help us build emotional resilience by forcing us to fail quickly but painlessly. They can accomplish the same thing in learning environments, and because we still call these learning events "games," we can protect our self-esteem, and give ourselves more permission to fail.

- The reason quick deaths and instant respawns are so prevalent in video games is because every minute of the game is assessing a player's skill. Contrary to traditional education, which tries to separate learning and assessment events, games recognize they can and should coexist.

POP QUIZ

Pro-Sports Edition

Some people devote their entire careers to trying and failing in a game. A handful of these people even reach a point where others will pay good money to watch them play. Yet it's important to realize that even within this elite cadre of professional athletes (i.e., professional game-players), you will see some of the highest failure rates of all time. See if you can guess the right failure statistics from some of the world's most successful athletes.

BABE RUTH SET A RECORD FOR MOST HOME RUNS IN A SINGLE SEASON. WHAT OTHER RECORD DID HE ALSO SET *THAT SAME SEASON*?

- **a)** Most bases stolen
- **b)** Most strikeouts
- **c)** Most umpires punched
- **d)** Most Ken Burns documentary features

Answer: In the midst of all his home run success, Babe Ruth also **struck out the most**. In fact, he led the league in strikeouts in five separate seasons. He said that every strike brought him closer to the next home run. In other words, he wasn't afraid to fail. (He also did punch an umpire.[12])

HOW MANY SHOTS DID MICHAEL JORDAN MISS IN HIS CAREER?

a) Zero
b) Less than 70
c) Over 2,500
d) Over 9,000

Answer: Yes, even the great Michael Jordan missed thousands of shots. "I've missed **more than 9,000 shots** in my career," he said. "I've lost almost 300 games. 26 times, I've been trusted to take the game winning shot and missed. I've failed over and over and over again in my life. And that is why I succeed."[13]

IN WHAT PERCENTAGE OF GAMES DO PROFESSIONAL BASEBALL PLAYERS MAKE A MISTAKE?

a) Less than 1%
b) 20%
c) 70%
d) 99.99%

Answer: There have been over 220,000 games in the history of baseball. Of those, only 23 were "perfect games" (where one team didn't let a single person from the other team reach first base).[14] 23 out of 220,000. That means professional ball players—people who are paid to be the best—still mess up in over **99.99%** of the games they play.

WAYNE GRETZKY, ONE OF THE GREATEST HOCKEY PLAYERS OF ALL TIME, SAID WHICH OF THE FOLLOWING?

a) *"You miss 100% of the shots you don't take."*
b) *"You only make 17% of the shots you **do** take."*

Answer: The answer is "A," but divide Gretzky's career goals (894) by his career shots taken (5,088) and you get a little over 17%, so he might as well have said "B" too. Obviously, Gretzky's point is not to focus on your success rate, but to *keep on shooting*.

Results from the pro-sports world seem pretty clear: We fail the most when we play.

6

OBSTACLES AND MAGIC CIRCLES

WOULD you like to play the World's Most Winnable Game? Thanks to Danish game designer Jesper Juul, now you can. I've shared Juul's game below, in its entirety. Here it is...

The World's Most Winnable Game also turns out to be The World's Least Enjoyable Game. As Juul pointed out after facetiously revealing his one-button game, "for something to be a good game, and a game at all, we expect resistance and the *possibility of failure*."[1]

Juul believes that games therefore contain a unique paradox. In almost every other part of life, we go to great lengths to *avoid* losing. And yet, when we play a game, we actually *want* to fail (at least a little bit).

So one of the reasons we fail the most when playing games is because—contrary to the rest of our life—we expect to fail. The game *requires* it. In order to be considered a game, something has to get in the player's way.

UNNECESSARY OBSTACLES

There are a lot of things we could add to spice up Juul's one-button game.

We could make it so a bunch of bad guys are guarding the button.

We could put the button in a really hard to reach place, like at the end of a maze.

We could add a bunch of tests or levels that you have to pass through before you're allowed to approach the button.

Basically, in order to turn this game into an *actual* game, we need to add in a bunch of obstacles. The objective stays the same (*push the button*), but all these extraneous challenges will make finally reaching and pushing that button a lot more fun.

Adding obstacles to a straightforward objective is essentially what game design is. In fact, this is exactly how philosopher Bernard Suits defined the concept of a "game."[2] He said:

> *Playing a game is a voluntary attempt to overcome unnecessary obstacles.*

Think about some of your favorite games: board games, mobile games, sports, you name it. All of them fit under this definition: there's a straightforward objective (capture the opponent's king, run the football into the end zone), that's complicated by a bunch of gratuitous barriers (you can only move a certain direction, there's a three-hundred-pound Defensive Tackle who's trying to stop you).

Perhaps no better game epitomizes unnecessary obstacles than golf. Comedian Robin Williams once imagined how golf was first invented, all those years ago in Scotland.[3] If you haven't seen this bit, it's worth it for the Scottish accent alone:

> *— Here's my idea for a f***ing sport. I knock a ball in a gopher hole.*
> *— Like pool?*
> *— F*** off pool. Not with a straight stick, with a little f***ed up stick. I whack a ball, it goes in a gopher hole.*
> *— Oh, you mean like croquet?*
> *— F*** croquet! I put the hole hundreds of yards away. Oh, f*** ya! Big fun, yeah!*
> *— Oh, like a bowling thing?*

> — F*** no! Not straight. I put s*** in the way. Like trees and bushes and high grass. So you can lose your f***ing ball. And go hacking away with a f***ing tire iron.

Golf certainly provides enough obstacles. But how many hurdles should a designer typically include in a game (or a game-based course)? Include too few obstacles and people get bored. Add too many and they get frustrated. Designers need to strike a delicate balance, and one that satisfies both skilled players as well as brand new ones.

If this sounds familiar to designing a learning environment, it should. And as you will see in the rest of this chapter, game designers have some special tools that we could take more advantage of in the education field.

CHASING GOLDILOCKS

Not too easy. Not too hard. When we design a game—or a learning course—we need to make the level of difficulty *just right*.

Those with education degrees may have studied this concept under the phrase "Zone of Proximal Development." A Soviet psychologist named Lev Vygotsky coined this term, and used it to argue that between what is known and what is unknown are things a learner can master through guidance and encouragement.

FAIL TO LEARN

You can call it the Zone of Proximal Development, but I just like to think of it as the "Goldilocks" zone.

How can we create environments that are "just right," ones that develop skills at a measured pace, while still keeping things engaging? Here's what game designers do: they draw a "magic circle" which captures the player in just the right spot.

DO YOU BELIEVE IN MAGIC?

> *The arena, the card-table, the magic circle, the temple, the stage, the screen, the tennis court, the court of justice, etc, are all in form and function play-grounds, i.e. forbidden spots, isolated, hedged round, hallowed, within which special rules obtain.[4]*
>
> JOHAN HUIZINGA

Picture this: You and a friend are having a conversation. Between the two of you is a checkerboard, though the two of you aren't using it. As your friend talks, she idly fiddles with the checkers. She moves them from square to square. She gathers them up and lets them tumble between her fingers.

Sounds like a perfectly innocent way to pass the time while talking with a friend.

Now imagine the two of you decide to play a game of checkers while you talk. Suddenly, your friend's fiddling isn't so innocent. There are rules she must follow. She can touch her own checker pieces, but she can't touch yours. And even when she touches her own, there are limits to how many she can touch, and where she can move them.

Imagine that, even though the two of you had agreed to play a game, your friend is still too wrapped up in the conversation. She continues to scoot around random pieces as she talks. At one point, she grabs one of your checkers and flicks it off the board. Even though she's acting the same way, the fact that you had agreed to "play a game" would suddenly make this behavior infuriating.

The reason you'd get frustrated is because when you agreed to play the game, you entered into what designers call the "magic circle."

The "magic circle" represents a boundary that every person crosses when they begin to play a game. Different rules apply inside of a magic circle. Sometimes entirely different realities apply. A magic circle might dictate how you move, what you say, or even what kind of person you are (a banker, a wizard, a supersonic hedgehog, etc.).

WHEN MAGIC CIRCLES OVERLAP, THINGS START TO GET WEIRD...

Johan Huizinga came up with the term "magic circle" in 1955, and the concept really took off fifty years later, thanks to Eric Zimmerman and Katie Salen and their book *Rules of Play*.

Zimmerman and Salen describe how the concept of a magic circle can "define a powerful space, investing its authority in the actions of players and creating new and complex meanings that are only possible in the space of play."[5]

Preserving the magic circle is a sacred part of every formal and informal game. It's what gives us the rules and realities we use to play with others. It can also help us figure out what we should *learn* inside of a game.

PUSHING THE BOUNDARY

Let's go back to that imaginary game of checkers, where you and your friend had agreed to play, and—stepping into the magic circle together—agreed to follow the normal checkers rules.

This time, let's pretend that your friend is notoriously terrible at checkers. She still wants to play, but you know that, in order for the game to last longer than thirty seconds, you'll have to go easy on her.

What do you do in this situation? You'd probably make a few wrong moves on purpose. Perhaps you play a bit of a game with yourself, trying to capture as few of her pieces as possible. In other words, you'd stretch the magic circle borders of this particular game. In addition to playing by the classic rules, you're now also playing by a set of personal rules—ones you created to give yourself a *new* challenge to learn from.

While every game has a magic circle, the boundaries of that circle can always be stretched. In fact, it's very important for players to be able to stretch boundaries when they play. That's why golf has handicaps, or why video games have things like side missions and cheat codes. We follow shared rules in a game, but we also can set our own rules to maximize our skill development.

We even can extend our magic circles to help us learn about social relationships. Let's say that checkers-playing friend of yours is going through a hard time in her life (maybe that's why she couldn't stop fiddling with the pieces). Perhaps instead of playing a normal game, you secretly choose to let her win. You've stretched the boundaries again: the goal isn't about winning, nor is it about trying to challenge yourself. It's become an interpersonal goal: you want to make your friend happy.

Here's why all this talk of circles is important. First, we in the education world need to pay attention to the magic circles we draw within learning environments. Just like in a game, a classroom is a special space. Certain rules and relationships apply that might be different from the rest of reality.

Second, we should recognize that if we draw our initial borders wide enough, then learners can do the fine-tuning and adjusting to create their own "Goldilocks Zone" of personal development. The student who finishes an activity early might choose to help coach a slower peer. The worker who needs a bit more time with the material might choose to take a quiz again, even though they technically got a passing score.

What rules exist within the magic circle of your courses? How do the boundaries you've drawn encourage exploration and growth? What about trying and failing? Have you created a safe enough environment that learners can playfully fail on purpose, or try to invent entirely new ways of winning? Can your students come up with new ways to prove their knowledge?

> *Miles sat across from Ms. Calleros, who showed him a piece of paper. The paper happened to be the latest quiz, and it had a big 0% written on it in red ink.*

> *The quiz belonged to Miles.*
>
> *"A zero," Miles said, momentarily at a loss for words. He furrowed his brow but then let out a small sigh of relief. "Few more of those, you'd probably have to kick me out of here, huh? Maybe I'm just not right for this school."*
>
> *Ms. Calleros shifted in her seat, never taking her eyes off Miles. "If a person wearing a blindfold picked the answers on a true-or-false quiz at random, do you know what score they would get?"*
>
> *"Uhh, fifty percent," Miles said. Then it dawned on him. "Wait—"*
>
> *The teacher smiled and nodded. "That's right!" she said. "Very sharp! On a true-or-false quiz, the only way to get all the answers wrong is to know which answers are right."*
>
> *Then Miles watched as Ms. Calleros reached into a drawer, grabbed a red pen, and changed the 0% on the quiz to a 100%*[6]
>
> EXCERPT FROM *SPIDER-MAN: INTO THE SPIDER-VERSE*

CHOOSE YOUR OWN ADVENTURE

Katie Salen and Eric Zimmerman provide a great definition of the word "play."[7]

> *Play is free movement within a more rigid structure.*

I like this simple definition because it helps us understand what the purpose of the "magic circle" really is. The magic circle *is* the "rigid structure" that Salen and Zimmerman are talking about. It is the hard boundary that we all agree to cross over when we enter a game. The magic circle helps us define the rules and agreements we make with other players.

But once these outer boundaries have been agreed upon, we are free to "play" however we'd like. And of course, depending on the circumstances, we might even stretch the "official" boundary of the magic circle to reach our own Goldilocks Zone. We give extra strikes to the smaller kids during the family baseball game, even though everyone's supposed to get three. We let our non-gaming older brother fumble with the Xbox controls instead of killing him like the rules of combat say to do (thanks, Collin).

One athlete had a particularly freeing and meaningful experience of play. During an international race in 2012, the leading runner got confused as to where the finish line was, and stopped running early. The athlete behind him realized his competitor's mistake and slowed down while pointing toward the actual finish. Most were impressed by this show of sportsmanship, except for the second-place finisher's coach. "The gesture has made him a better person, but not a better athlete," the coach said.[8]

What this second-place finisher experienced was a moment of freedom within the larger structure of a "game." He bent the traditional rules (*"run as fast as you can"*) in order to develop a skill that he felt was much more important.

Within the larger "rigid structure" of your educational setting, what sort of free movement do you offer your learners? And do they see this free movement as an invitation to play?

One way to answer this question is to consider what type of goal your rigid structure is pushing learners toward. Jesper Juul explains that most challenges point toward one of the following three goals. Since Juul kicked off this chapter, I thought it only fitting to end with him too.

Take a look at his goal types, and think about how they relate to your own educational settings. Knowing which kind of goal you've set for your learners will give you a better idea of how to open up more freedoms within.

- **A completable goal**: This describes the linear objectives of a game like *Super Mario Brothers*. But it can also describe how a learner completes a one-time course like Chemistry 101. Once you've passed the exam (or saved the princess, as the case may be), you will always be someone who's completed this feat. And it's unlikely (especially for a 101 course) that you'll go back through it again.

- **A transient goal**: Other challenges are designed to be "won" repeatedly. This could be anything from a game of *Solitaire* to a soccer match. In the Learning and Development world, an annual compliance course would have a transient goal. You complete it to get certified for a year, but you'll be back in this same course again soon.

- **An improvement goal**: Games with improvement goals are all about beating your personal best. As you play over and over, you develop more skills, and you reach the game's objectives faster. There's lasting benefit to designing courses this way. As Juul explains, "Such improvement goals concern our ongoing personal struggles for improvement, and can by definition never be reached."[9]

CHAPTER SUMMARY

- In order for games to be "fun," they have to include an element of failure. Enjoyment comes from overcoming "unnecessary obstacles."

- Whether designing a game or a learning course, aim for the Zone of Proximal Development (or the "Goldilocks Zone"), ensuring that your obstacles are neither too easy to overcome, nor too difficult. When they have enough freedom to do so, learners can actually help stretch "official" rules one way or the other to reach their personal Goldilocks Zone.

- Every game has a "magic circle" that can contain everything from official rules to social and cultural norms. When you step into a magic circle, you are agreeing to obey a shared rulebook, or shared reality. Magic circles are "safe" because they're insulated from the outside world. That usually also means that it's okay to fail inside a magic circle, because there will be no repercussions in the real world.

- Course designers can overlap several goal types and ways to win in their learning environments. They can include everything from official rules to social rules to completable, transient, or improvement goals.

III. THEREFORE, GAMES ARE THE BEST WAY FOR PEOPLE TO LEARN

7

THE FIRST STEP TO GAMIFYING

IN 2002, MICROSOFT LAUNCHED "XBOX LIVE," a subscription service that let video game players across the world connect to play games together online. Other gaming consoles had similar programs, but Microsoft's was unique in that it charged players an annual fee.

To stay competitive, Microsoft decided to "gamify" their paid subscription. They created an "Xbox Live Rewards" program, which let people earn "Microsoft Points" for doing things like completing surveys or making purchases.

A few years later, the Xbox Live Rewards program was still going strong, so Microsoft came up with a new idea. They started giving people 20 Microsoft Points on their birthday, as a fun way to say thanks.

Strangely, some people did not appreciate this birthday present.

Why? What could possibly be wrong with giving someone free Microsoft Points one day of the year?

Probably because 20 Microsoft Points equates to a whopping $0.25.

"Wow a whole 20 Microsoft points is what Microsoft gave me for my birthday," one user posted.

"Microsoft has sent me the best birthday gift I've ever received. 20 Microsoft Points. TWENTY. That's $0.25. Thanks guys ;)" said another.[1]

The Xbox Rewards program has since been redesigned, but there are some important lessons to learn from this less-than-happy-birthday. There's nothing wrong with gamifying through points, but when Microsoft tried to connect their points to something that people valued on a deeper level (their once-a-year special day), they ended up exposing the superficiality of their own gamified system.

IT'S NOT ABOUT THE POINTS

People don't care about how many points they own. What they care about is feeling honored for their continued loyalty. Other gamified approaches have the same kind of hidden meaning. There's no market value for a Girl Scout badge. The value comes from having this token from a special club that broadcasts to other members the unique efforts you've taken.

In other words, it's easy to gamify something. There are hundreds of tidbits you can drop into just about anything.

What's hard is figuring out what that game element is supposed to make your audience *feel* and *do*.

Here's the good news: we've spent this whole book isolating two core elements of gamification, and understanding why and how people utilize them to take action and get results. Now we'll see how to put these two elements into practice.

The rest of this chapter will give you several examples of how to employ elements of failure and play within learning environments. You should be able to add these to just about any piece of instructional content. Most are low-cost and easy to implement within existing courses. As you review these, think about which ones might help your learner groups get the most comfortable with the concept of failure and play.

Welcome to the actionable portion of this manifesto. This can be your kid-in-a-candy-store moment. You already know the deeper motivations and results of failing and playing. Now you get to pick out some favorite tools to trigger these responses. These are the tiny, gamified sparks that you'll fan into flames.

GAMIFYING WITH FAILURE

Include a "replay" button

This might be one of the easiest ways to de-escalate fears of failure. Make sure students can *go back*. This could be as simple as adding a "replay" button to an online course, or making sure linked videos can be played through as often as someone would like, at any point they wish.

But you could also go one layer deeper and use this concept within any quiz or exam setting. To do this, you might have to argue with your stakeholders why it's okay to let students retake an exam after failing (hopefully, the information from the earlier chapters will help you win this argument). Think about it this way: A learner fails a test, and instead of giving up, they actually *want* to try again. Why wouldn't we want to encourage this? Why wouldn't we want to put "replay" or "redo" buttons *everywhere*?

Use humor to deescalate fears of failure

Players love killing their avatar in *Super Monkey Ball* 2, even more than they love winning the game. Consider using humor to show learners it's okay (and even funny) to make mistakes. Most of the gamified examples I've seen of this have some form of over-the-top deaths of cartoon characters. I don't know what that says about designers' sense of humor, but hey, whatever works.

Let learners socialize their mistakes

Instead of focusing discussion around the right answers, let learners spend a larger portion of time discussing what they got *wrong*. After all, this does more than just build group cohesion and social learning. It also helps you identify common missteps and assumptions students are making. Instructors who only focus on reviewing the right answer are missing an important opportunity.

Incentivize losing

This may not be the best thing to do on an annual or summative exam. But for lower-stakes tests or check-ins, consider encouraging learners to fail on purpose. Give out a prize for the most questions answered wrong (and remember, usually the only way to get *every* question wrong is to know which answers are right).

Many industries have found playful ways to incentivize and gamify failure. The Bulwer Lytton Fiction Contest gives an annual prize to whoever can write the *worst* opening sentence to a novel (see Notes for the latest winner).[2] And of course Hollywood has The Golden Raspberry Awards (also known as the "Razzies") to honor the worst films of the year.

Fun fact: Sandra Bullock once won a Razzie in the

very same year she won an Oscar. The 2010 Razzie was for her performance in the movie *All About Steve* (which currently has a 6% rating on Rotten Tomatoes),[3] while she took home an Oscar in that same year for her role in *The Blind Side*.[4]

Even A-List celebrities are getting on board with gamified failure.

Provide clear, low-level punishments to compartmentalize failure

A big problem with failure is that people assume it reflects a personal inadequacy, rather than a normal step to learning. To help combat this, design your courses so that it's clear what each failure will "cost" a participant.

But remember: Failure "costs" in traditional training are often much too high. Don't penalize learners by making them redo the whole course. Instead, here are a few gamified ways to build low-level punishments into your material:

- **Power/health meters**: These can incrementally decrease until a "life" is lost. You also can offer the option to refill or "power-up" these meters along the way.

- **Resources**: Learners can collect (and then risk losing) things like tokens, coins, in-game property, etc. Failure can "cost" a set amount, or you can involve an element of random chance (*"Guess wrong and you'll lose anywhere from one to three coins..."*).

- **Time**: Imagine a test where instead of needing to pass with 80%, you simply have to reach the end screen before a timer hits 00:00. Perhaps every wrong answer means a 10-second runoff. This is simply another way to conceptualize punishment, but notice here how learners will stop thinking about preserving their final score, and instead give themselves more permission to try and fail as they work to simply reach the end.

Put the hard problems up front

In an earlier chapter, we saw studies that showed the benefits of letting students struggle. Facing complex, high-level problems right off the bat actually strengthened students' overall performance. Even wording questions to be deliberately confusing doesn't seem to stop them from learning through this deliberate struggle. So instead of ratcheting up difficulty in the typical stairstep approach, consider giving learners something really hard right at the beginning. The early failure might frustrate them, but it will also teach them to get used to the idea of making mistakes.

Include confidence ratings

This is another easy add-on to existing course material. If you already have a test designed, consider adding a "confidence rating" beside each question. As we've seen, the more confident you are in an answer that ends up being wrong, the more likely you are to remember the correct response in the future.

Make feedback *immediate*

Technology has certainly helped us score and distribute test results quicker. But we can still get better at giving more immediate feedback, even in digital learning environments. Janet Metcalfe's research into error-based learning supports this claim. She explains that students "pay attention to the feedback when it is given immediately. However, their interest flags with a long delay."[5]

Think back to how those Perceptual Learning Models (like the art history one) were designed. The learner got correct/incorrect feedback *after every question*. Most course design software is built to give quiz results only after the end of the quiz. As a designer or teacher, consider breaking the mold here, and give students feedback on a question-by-question basis instead.

GAMIFYING WITH PLAY

Recall Katie Salen and Eric Zimmerman's definition of play: *"free movement within a more rigid structure."* Play-based gamification is therefore unique. In order to encourage free movement, the thing you add might be what creates (or at least contributes to) the "rigid structure." Think about which of these elements you could add to the structures of your existing materials.

Give learners choices

This may seem obvious, but you'd be surprised how many educational and training courses don't offer a *single choice* to learners. They're expected to sit still and listen, and then facilitators wonder why no one is having any fun.

Conversely, wherever learners *do* have choice, that is usually where you'll see them playing the most. I think about the interactive, online quizzes I've delivered within a classroom setting. Whenever I let learners come up with their own nicknames on the quiz screen, I see them having *way* too much fun with it. People seem to pay more attention to the inside jokes and acronyms than the actual quiz answers. Why? Perhaps because it was the one spot where they had the freedom to choose.

I never would have thought something like typing in your name could be fun, but when it's one of the few places they have to exercise freedom, you'd better believe people will find a way to make it engaging. And the more engagement you create, the more opportunities for learning that you have.

So even if you're stuck having to teach a rigid, mandated curriculum, there are still ways to offer freedom of choice. Just remember that wherever a mandate exists, play will not. As James Carse says in his book, *Finite and Infinite Games*:

"(I)f they *must* play, they cannot *play*."[6]

Make "bendy" rules

What happens in your course when a learner finds a different solution than the one you have in mind? Do you shoot them down because it's not the "right" right answer? Or do you use it as an opportunity to explore options, think outside the box, or maybe even update the material? Nothing shuts down playful thinking faster than the response, "Well, that's not *technically* wrong, but..."

If learners suspect you're only looking for one specific answer, chances are you won't have a very playful or collaborative environment.

I think one of the reasons professional sports are so entertaining is because occasionally teams will find a new way to bend the rules. American football owes many of its innovations (and trick plays) to the legendary coach Glenn Scobey "Pop" Warner.[7] Pop Warner was always looking for ways to play *just* inside the rules of the game. For example, after realizing the rules allowed for players to wear elbow pads, Warner had a special set made for his team. The pads were designed to look like a football when the player crossed his arms, making it impossible for the defense to know who to chase.[8]

And speaking of chasing...

Include physical activity

Play researcher Dr. Stuart Brown calls physical movement "perhaps the most basic form of play."[9] Incorporating physical activity is also a great litmus test for course designers, to see how open they really are to playing in a classroom.

How often do you encourage learners to stand up or shake out their limbs? Have you ever asked people in a classroom to get up and switch seats? And why are we willing to do these things more when teaching children than when teaching adults? Have you ever encouraged people to get up and move when teaching an online or pre-recorded course? And if you haven't, what would it take to get over this discomfort and start recognizing the tangible benefits of physical play?

Just about any sort of activity can boost your physical resilience. Dr. Jane McGonigal found that even a few minutes of sitting still can cause your body to shut down at a metabolic level, which can negatively impact everything from your immune system to your ability to handle stress.[10] So if we want to have engaged, healthy learners, one of the most directly impactful things we can do is to simply have them move around.

Incentivize exploration

I have a favorite way of introducing a new tool, system, or piece of software to a group of learners. I invite them to try to break it on purpose. Everyone loves this assignment, not only because it feels devious, but because it activates their playful sense of exploration. There are no "correct steps" to follow, and no manuals to consult. All they need to complete this task is a playful sense of curiosity (okay, and perhaps a little bit of deviousness as well). And of course, as learners poke and prod the new tool looking for a weak spot, they're also learning how it works.

This type of exploratory play is used in many game environments. Think about the open worlds of *Minecraft* or *Grand Theft Auto*. Part of the fun of playing these games is exploring the extensively detailed alternate reality.

Another way that games encourage exploration is to hide "Easter eggs" within their virtual worlds. Similar to traditional Easter eggs, a game Easter egg usually contains a little prize, joke, or bit of extra content.[11] The classic video game *NBA Jam* contained a secret code that allowed people to play as characters who weren't exactly pro basketball players. You could pick people like The Beastie Boys, The Fresh Prince of Bel-Air, and even Bill Clinton.[12]

Oftentimes, the joy of *searching* for these Easter eggs is even greater than the prize itself.

Take a play history

Here's another tip from Dr. Brown for those trying to play more: take a personal "play history." Brown explains that creating a play history can give you "a guide to free-flowing empowerment."[13] Most instructional designers already know that interviewing their audience is an essential precursor to building a course. What better way to listen, bond, and empathize with your audience than asking them to describe how they play and have fun?

This idea of a play history can also align with the concept of personality styles or player types. One such taxonomy comes from Richard Bartle, who introduced his four types of game players in 1996.[14] If you don't know this four-type profile, see if you can figure out which one you are. Then see if you can identify what types appear most often in your learner groups.

- **The Socializer**: This person plays games to interact with the people around them. They're less interested in the game itself, and more interested in the collaborations, conversations, and relationships between everyone who's playing.

- **The Explorer**: This type of person really values the freedom to wander through a game and discover things on their own. Easter eggs (which we talked about earlier) are great to use with Explorers.

- **The Achiever**: This type of person likes to see (and show off) their accomplishments. Things like badges and other progressive tokens are great game incentives for Achievers. In the real world, this might take the form of promotions, new job titles, or the corner office.

- **The Killer**: And finally, there are "Killers." Killers also like achievements and accomplishments, but for them to call something a "win," it means others have to have lost. Killers can also enjoy creating chaos in the system, or pushing the boundaries or rules of the game. The assignment "break this new tool" appeals to the Killer type best.

There are many player and personality types out there, and many excellent resources explain how to use them. For those new to gamification, my advice is to simply consider asking a player-type question as part of your "play history" analysis. Consider describing the types above, and asking your audience which one speaks to them.

Give them something "impossible"

I remember deciding sometime in late middle school that I wasn't going to pursue a career in math. My (uneducated) reason was this: Why spend time trying to come up with answers that my teacher already knows? I figured that, at least in my humanities classes, I could invent new and creative interpretations that no one had ever worded the same way before.

This very naive perspective of mine should get you thinking about what your learners believe. Do they think their instructors already know all the answers? And if so, what's the point of them trying that hard?

What would happen if you added some "impossible to solve" questions to your material, or—if nothing else— got comfortable answering questions with *"I don't know the answer to that. What do you think?"*

The makers of early computer games often used this "impossibility" element in their design. "(We were) never expected to be able to complete our own games," explains UK developer Ste Pickford. "We just presumed that some expert player out there might be good enough to get to the end."[15]

It's a shame my younger self wasn't aware of the rich history of unsolved problems in the field of mathematics. Isaac Newton wrote his famous *Philosophiae Naturalis Principia Mathematica* (which explained the principles of time, force, and motion) because a peer had made a 40 shilling bet that no one could do it.[16] And in 2000, the Clay Mathematics Institute unveiled their "Millennium Problems," seven seemingly unsolvable math stumpers. Each solution is worth a cool one million dollars, and so far, only one of the seven has been solved.[17]

Let's see...gambling bets, recognition, reward money, impossible obstacles. It turns out the field of mathematics is rife with playful gamification mechanics. Just like everything else.

CHAPTER SUMMARY

- Gamified learning that stems from the concept of failure: replay buttons, using humor in fail-states, socializing mistakes, incentivizing loss, providing compartmentalized punishments, giving hard problems up front, using confidence ratings, and dispensing immediate feedback.

- Gamified learning that stems from the concept of play: giving learners choices, making "bendy" rules, incorporating physical activity, incentivizing exploration, taking a "play history," and giving learners something "impossible."

A GAMIFIED POP QUIZ

I thought I'd put my money where my mouth is. Here is a pop quiz (mostly just general trivia)[18] that incorporates several of the failure and play game elements I mention above. Give it a try, and see if you notice a change in your interest or level of engagement with this quiz, compared to the others.

Instructions:

- AVOID PICKING THE RIGHT ANSWERS. No one has ever been able to achieve a 0% score on their first try—can you? There is only one correct answer to each question, so you have a three-in-four chance of successfully answering wrong.
- For each question, rank on a scale of 1-10 how confident you are that you've successfully picked a wrong answer.
- You can attempt for a 0% score as many times as you want. Write your letter choices on a piece of paper, then have someone else check

them against the answer key on the following page. If they say you got one or more questions right, then try again.

1. WHICH WAS THE FIRST TOY TO APPEAR ON A TELEVISION COMMERCIAL?

   a) Mr. Potato Head
   b) Play-Doh
   c) Hula Hoop
   d) Magic Eight Ball

Confidence: __

2. HOW LONG DID THE "HUNDRED YEARS WAR" LAST?

   a) 76 years
   b) 92 years
   c) 100 years
   d) 116 years

Confidence: __

3. HOW MANY TRIBUTARIES DOES THE AMAZON HAVE?

   a) 1
   b) 101
   c) 1,100
   d) 11,000

FAIL TO LEARN

Confidence: __

4. WHICH LETTER WAS MOST RECENTLY ADDED TO THE ENGLISH ALPHABET?

    a) G
    b) J
    c) X
    d) Z

Confidence: __

5. WHICH OF THESE PLANETS ROTATES CLOCKWISE?

    a) Mercury
    b) Venus
    c) Earth
    d) Mars

Confidence: __

6. SIT STILL FOR THE NEXT THREE MINUTES.

That means in order to get this question wrong, you have to get up and do something physically active. Stretch your arms above your head. Stand up. Do a jumping jack. The clock is ticking!

Confidence: __

Answer Key (showing *right* answers):

1) a, 2) d, 3) c, 4) b, 5) b, 6) Only way to get this question *right* is to sit still!

Failure and Play Elements Used:

- "Replay" button (unlimited attempts)
- Incentivizing loss
- Confidence ratings
- Compartmentalizing punishment (only a 25% chance of getting an answer "wrong")
- Immediate feedback (answer key immediately provided)
- "Bendy" rules (honor-system grading)
- Incorporating physical activity

8

THE "FAIL TO LEARN" GAMIFICATION MODEL

THE ELEMENTS in the previous chapter are all quick and easy ways to bring game design to your educational material. This chapter will go one step further by suggesting a very basic framework for doing this on a larger scale. It's meant for those who want to enhance reactions to failure and play across an entire curriculum or organization.

I'm keeping this chapter short on purpose because I'm already worried about overcomplicating things. As you've seen, we don't need elaborate models. The essence of gamification basically boils down to this:

- To gamify something, you must create *unnecessary obstacles* for players.

- In order to deal with "unnecessary obstacles," players must have a healthy relationship with failure and play.

- Play lets us see game obstacles as "unnecessary," because we have the freedom to choose how we engage with these challenges.

- Failure lets us experience frustration or disappointment when we fail to overcome an obstacle, but also resilience and hope as we adjust and try again.

- When you gamify through failure and play, you are tapping into the core motivators for why we engage with and learn from something.

That's about it, which means we should start small when we think about a "gamified framework." You don't need much to create an effective, engaging system. That's why the "Fail to Learn" model starts with this:

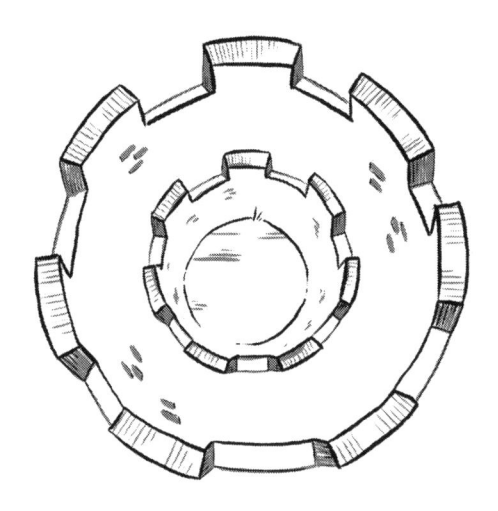

See what I did there? It may not look like much, but I just took the "magic circle" we discussed earlier, and fancied it up a bit...and then I cut a hole in its center.

Why make the magic circle into a ring? As designers of serious learning environments, we have to recognize the difference between people on the *outside* (those wanting to develop individual skills) and the people on the *inside* (those wanting to solve existing problems). The "magic ring" separates these two groups. People must pass through the magic environment—with its unique rules and realities—to get to the other side.

Here's how the two groups—the course Learners and the course Designers—pass through our model:

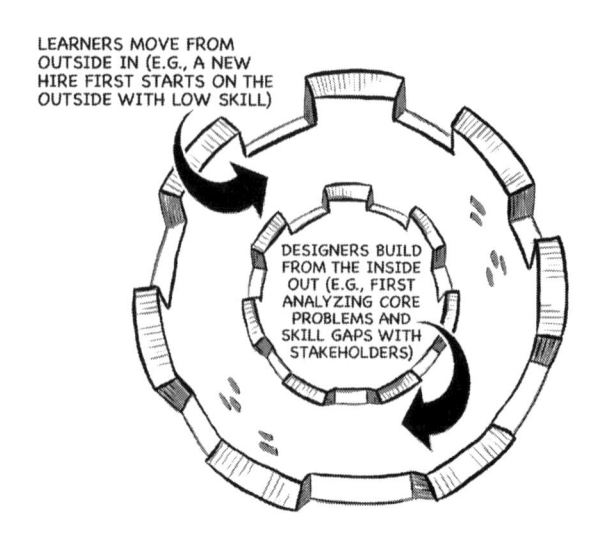

LEARNERS MOVE FROM OUTSIDE IN (E.G., A NEW HIRE FIRST STARTS ON THE OUTSIDE WITH LOW SKILL)

DESIGNERS BUILD FROM THE INSIDE OUT (E.G., FIRST ANALYZING CORE PROBLEMS AND SKILL GAPS WITH STAKEHOLDERS)

As a designer, you fill the center of the circle with the real-world behaviors learners must do to solve a core problem. That's another reason why we had to cut out the center. In a serious learning environment, the actions and behaviors in the center are real-world problems. We've separated them from all the bright-faced, first-day learners wandering around on the outside, but these real-world problems also don't have the luxury of existing in the magic circle portion of our material. And as a designer, you always want to start with the real-world problems you're solving, before you move into your gamified alternate realities.

Let's pause here and look at an example. Say a company wants new customer service training to reduce the number of complaints they get. You'll draw a "magic ring," and start in the center by listing all the observable actions a learner will perform on the job that will directly result in a reduced number of complaints.

Another thing about the center part of your circle: It should involve as many stakeholders, subject-matter-experts, and front-line workers as possible. Think of this center space as a community of the knowledgeable and the newly trained.

This centerpiece should be a place of constant discussion, between everyone from administrators to recently trained employees or graduated students. This is a place to exchange ideas and ultimately create better, new ways to analyze and solve an organization's problems.

I like to think of this center part as a "Guild."

THE GUILD
PEER-BASED COMMUNITY TO ADD TO AND ANALYZE
THE TOPIC FOR CONTINUING DEVELOPMENT.

Moving outward to the second layer of our model—this is where the fun happens. After all, it's what's left of our magic circle. It's the game environment. It's the actions and exercises. I like to think of it as a "gauntlet" that learners pass through on their way from being unskilled in a particular area to being able to sit at the table of experts, as part of the Guild.

There's a lot more to say about this middle part, but let's just get it labeled for now.

THE GAUNTLET
GAMIFIED LEARNING EXPERIENCES THAT ARE HIGH-FAILURE AND PLAY-ORIENTED.

Here's what's unique about the Gauntlet. It's all experiential action, all the time. The challenges are as "real" as possible, meaning they try to mimic the real-world behaviors that Guild-members are performing daily. Feedback within the Gauntlet is immediate, meaning results come quick, just like they do in real life.

The Gauntlet is gamified, experiential learning. But because it's still a training environment, learners are safe to try and fail as often as they'd like. The feedback may be quick, but it's relatively painless. Learners also have freedom to fully explore the boundaries of the Gauntlet, and even try out some novel solutions to the challenges it presents. Meanwhile Guild members are watching carefully from within, seeing who has used this freedom and creative leeway to come up with previously unthought-of solutions.

The Gauntlet is where you can add in all sorts of different gamified elements. These could be things we've discussed already like physical activity, power meters, or timers. But they can also include other common game mechanics like points, battles, maps, or avatars. Remember to add these a little at a time! Because the "Fail to Learn" model is already built to encourage failure and play, you won't need too many bells and whistles to keep learners engaged.

No matter what you include in the Gauntlet (levels! narratives! villains!), one thing will be surprisingly absent. And learners will probably notice this absence right away.

There are no lectures in the Gauntlet.

No slide decks.

No manuals, charts, or scripts to memorize.

Other than perhaps a basic set of rules for playing,

the Gauntlet contains no passive information about the content you're supposed to learn.

Thank goodness learners entering the Gauntlet are told it's okay to fail in here, because with this lack of information, what else do they have to rely on. Their wits? Their critical thinking? That might be enough for some, but others will no doubt fail in the face of these difficult, game-based challenges. And after failing a few times in a row, learners might actually be craving those dry, boring manuals.

So here's the final part of our model:

THE TEMPLES
SELF-SOUGHT INFORMATION, DESIGNED FOR MULTIPLE MEDIA TYPES AND LEARNING STYLES.

The "Temples" represent all of the information and didactic instruction that might go into a traditional course. A Temple may represent an expert willing to lecture on a topic, or it might represent a resource library where someone who doesn't like to sit through lectures can go to read by themselves until they feel ready to step into the Gauntlet again. There can be many Temples, and Temples might overlap for different courses. The important thing is that the *learner should seek out the Temple*, instead of being forced to absorb every piece of content in every medium.

Let's say our example company hires someone brand new, and this person needs to learn the basics of customer service to help decrease the overall number of complaints (the business objective). On their first day of training, they immediately enter the Gauntlet, where they're bombarded with fake phone calls from confused, belligerent "customers." This otherwise stressful situation is softened by several gamified elements, including the use of humor, levels of difficulty, and "extra lives." Even still the new hire quickly realizes that they need help if they expect to make it through.

One thing they need is a simple explanation of how the company's phone system works. The new hire "exits" the magical, contained world of the Gauntlet, and finds several Temples of information that can help them. There's a New Hire Mentor who holds office hours every afternoon. There's a video in the company intranet showing how to operate the phone. There's even a full phone manual that they could read through if they really wanted to.

Similar Temples of information exist for everything from soft skills to product descriptions. When the new hire feels ready, they enter the Gauntlet once more, knowing they're free to come back out and pick up more information as they need it.

A "BACK OF THE NAPKIN" TRAINING MODEL

That's it. That's about as elaborate as we'll get with the "Fail to Learn" model:

- **Step One**: Form a "Guild" to define your real-world behaviors (and the skills needed to perform them at an acceptable level).

- **Step Two**: Use gamified elements to create a "Gauntlet," in which playful failure is abundant and information is scarce. Throw your new learners into the Gauntlet right on their first day.

- **Step Three**: Take all the information and expert sources on how to develop the needed skills, and organize them into "Temples" that learners can self-seek whenever they choose to emerge from the Gauntlet. You might have to create new pieces of information, but usually, there's an abundance of people, presentations, and documents just waiting to be used.

You'll notice that this barebones training framework borrows from many of the successful studios we reviewed earlier. Japan and Singapore's education systems do something similar in the way they let students struggle through questions on their own (a mini-gauntlet) before finally stepping back to review with their teachers (those "temples" of information).

This is also how anyone learns to play literally any sport. Okay, maybe there's a few weirdos who want to read the official rulebook of basketball before stepping onto the court, but for the vast majority of us, our first action is to enter the Gauntlet and just start dribbling and shooting. It's only after we tire ourselves out (and realize we're not a natural) that we start seeking the coaches, videos, and pro tips.

What drives this whole model is the dual-cylinder engine of failure and play. The more learners are allowed to freely and playfully fail, the more they pinpoint the information they're missing, and the more targeted they become in their self-education. In this way, the "Fail to Learn" model creates not only knowledgeable students, but empowered ones. And once these students have passed through the Gauntlet, the Guild turns them into active members of the learning and development community. They join a community of veterans, where they apply their skills to solve real-world problems, but also work together to update the Gauntlet and Temples for future generations.

CHAPTER SUMMARY

The "Fail to Learn" model is a back-of-the-napkin framework that can help people integrate failure and play throughout a whole curriculum or organization. The model is made up of:

- **Temples:** These are collected sources of information that *learners seek out themselves*. Temples can include different media types (lecture, slide decks, webinars, Q&A sessions, etc.) and learning styles to give learners a chance to select what works best for them.

- **The Gauntlet:** This is a gamified learning experience that is both high-failure and play oriented. While the Gauntlet is designed to be challenging (difficult problems with no information) it is also completely "safe," meaning learners should feel free to experiment and try different solutions, learning from their many mistakes. The Gauntlet can also incorporate other more "standard" game mechanics (like avatars, levels, or narratives) as designers see fit.

- **The Guild:** This is a peer-based community that includes everyone from stakeholders to front-line workers to recent "graduates." The Guild is a place for these people to review trainees' work and discuss new ways to develop and advance the material for future generations.

- To get a blank "Fail to Learn" template to sketch out ideas for your own course design, visit www.scottprovence.com/fail-to-learn

CONCLUSION

9

THE PLAYING HUMAN

> *(Games are) a trigger for adults to again become primitive, primal, as a way of thinking and remembering.*[1]
>
> SHIGERU MIYAMOTO

> *Many things we have fun at doing are in fact training us to be better cavemen.*[2]
>
> RAPH KOSTER

ONE OF THE first programs I ever designed was in partnership with a physics professor at the University of Washington. He had a unique approach to teaching his "Introduction to Astronomy" class. On the first day, he'd take students to the planetarium. And as they gazed up at an orbiting night sky, he'd tell them to imagine they're living ten thousand years in the past.

"Look at the weird path of that star," the professor would point out. "Why is it moving so differently than the rest of them?"

"It's a planet," someone would inevitably say.

"Ah, but it's ten thousand years ago, and you're a caveman," he'd reply. "You don't know anything about planets. You don't know about the solar system or elliptical orbits. Heck, it's not until after the mid-term that you're even allowed to know about gravity."

It usually got pretty quiet after that. Then the professor would ask again. "Looking with your Paleolithic eyes, how can you start to explain what you see?"

This is the approach we need to take when it comes to understanding and using gamification. We have so many modern-day tools at our fingertips that we're starting to lose track of the basics of instructional and motivational design. My goal in this manifesto was to take us back to our earliest gaming roots, so that we could clear away our preconceptions and with clear, instinctive thinking, ask "What's the best way for someone to learn?"

And as we've seen, gamifying learning is more than just one of the most effective ways to learn. It's also one of the earliest. In my opinion, we have games to thank for our survival as a species.

This manifesto was meant to help you reconnect with the essential elements that make us game-playing and always-learning humans. "Civilization arises and unfolds in and as play,"[3] said Dutch historian Johan Huizinga. Huizinga actually wanted to call us something other than Homo Sapiens, "the wise human." According to him, we are Homo Ludens, *"the playing human."*

When I gamify something, I like to think as a caveman. I put on my *Homo Ludens* tiger skin and I think about what feeling my learners will get in their gut when they fail. I picture how they will move through disbelief, perhaps even frustration, but ultimately, curiosity and an eagerness to try again. I picture their curiosity as I frame the borders of my magic circle, one that will keep them protected, but also allow for freedom of movement. Then I start to add my gamified elements, my fake tigers and targets so they can practice their aim.

I hope this manifesto has helped you get in touch with your own *Homo Ludens* roots. I hope that as you design your next course, you tap into the million years of motivational instincts buried inside you. I hope that when others try to critique your use of failure or play, you stand ready to explain just how far these two concepts have allowed us to come. I can't wait for you to show others how we learn the most through failure, and fail the most through games, and how it's only logical that games are one of the very best ways for us to learn.

The revolution is waiting for you. Your learners are waiting. Time to pick up your tiger skin and your spear and get to work.

THANK YOU

Thank you for reading *Fail to Learn*. If you enjoyed this book, and are interested in creating your own learning or game-based resources, visit www.scottprovence.com. There you can see how we turn content from experts like you into materials the whole world can enjoy.

You have something important to teach people, but they might not be paying attention. Our team uses a unique combination of instructional and game design to make your learning content bite-sized and engaging. We create measurable results so that people see *you* as their guide to personal success.

Go to www.scottprovence.com to see how it works, and to try out our free program-building tool. Thanks again for reading, and look forward to talking more soon!

ACKNOWLEDGMENTS

Writing a book is its own kind of lesson in failure. As with any project, there were a lot of times here that I wanted to give up. Fortunately, I'm surrounded by some incredibly smart and supportive people who provided everything from industry-specific knowledge to perfectly timed "suck it up" pep talks. It's because of them that this book made it, and while naming everyone who helped me would require a book of its own, I'd like to thank just a few of these people now.

For starters, I want to thank Will Burrows for his amazing illustrations and cover art. Will has an exceptional talent for bringing an idea in your head to life, and I've been fortunate to work with him in creating everything from children's books to self-help books. Will didn't bat an eye when I asked, "Is it possible to do something that looks like an edgy manifesto...but also like a back-of-the-napkin cartoon?" Thank you, Will, and here's to many more projects to come.

I also want to thank the many gamification and training experts that I've learned so much from over the years. Perhaps no two people have taught me more about this topic than Monica Cornetti and Jonathan Peters of Sententia Gamification. These two have created an amazing culture and community of learning professionals all dedicated to exploring how people learn through play. If you're looking for something else to read, or for your next certification course, check out Monica and Jonathan's amazing resources.

Huge thanks also goes to another gamification expert, Kerstin Oberprieler, for not only being a great sounding board for ideas but also for keeping me accountable to getting these ideas on the page. And of course, once the words were written, I had to find people who had industry expertise, as well as the courage to tell me the truth, and then pester these people with draft after draft of the book. Countless thanks to Robert Moon, Ceil Tilney, Joe Abittan, and Roxanne Walmsley for lending me their eagle eyes. Any coherent thoughts in this book are because of them—any mistakes or misstatements are entirely mine.

Finally, I want to thank three very special people who make this world such a gameful, joyful place. Jo is my partner in writing and in life, so of course it's from her that I've learned to publish (and live) fearlessly. Collin, my little brother, is not only a great game-playing partner, but he's also an incredibly talented educator, one who's teaching the next generation of students how to play, fail, and learn. And to Jane—one of the next generation's newest members—I can't wait to explore the world with you. It is to you three that this book is dedicated.

ABOUT THE AUTHOR

Scott Provence is an Instructional Designer and Technical Writer who specializes in gamification and narrative theory. His print, instructor-led, and web-based curricula have been delivered internationally and across all fifty states.

Scott received an MA in English and an MFA in Creative Writing from the University of Washington, where he was a Nelson Bentley Fellow and Webber Teaching Prize nominee. In 2019, Scott won Training

Magazine's award for Excellence in No-Tech or Low-Tech Gamification Design.

Scott enjoys working with teams at any stage and budget to create measurable and engaging gamified training solutions. You can find samples of his work, as well as free training resources, at www.scottprovence.com.

NOTES

1. Welcome to the Revolution

1. "Gamification Market." *Market Research Firm*, Mar. 2020, www.marketsandmarkets.com/Market-Reports/gamification-market-991.html.
2. Andre, Louie. "47 Gamification Statistics You Must Know." *Finances Online*, FinancesOnline.com, 9 Apr. 2020, financesonline.com/gamification-statistics/
3. A. Mora, D. Riera, C. Gonzalez and J. Arnedo-Moreno, "A Literature Review of Gamification Design Frameworks," *2015 7th International Conference on Games and Virtual Worlds for Serious Applications (VS-Games)*, Skovde, 2015, pp. 1-8.
4. CRMGamified. "Top 6 CRM Gamification Mistakes (And How to Avoid Them!)." *CRM Gamified*, 3 Mar. 2020, crmgamified.com/the-top-6-crm-gamification-mistakes/
5. Pelling, Nick. "The (short) prehistory of 'gamification'..." *Funding Startups (& other impossibilities)*, 9 August 2011, nanodome.wordpress.com/2011/08/09/the-short-prehistory-of-gamification/
6. Zajicek, Charlotte. "The history of auctions: from ancient Greece to online houses." *The Telegraph*, 7 October 2016, www.telegraph.co.uk/art/online-auctions/history-of-auctions/; Denton, Mitchell. "The History of Gamification - Journey from 1896 to the 21st Century." *Gamify*, www.gamify.com/gamification-blog/the-history-of-gamification;McEachern, Alex. "A History of Loyalty Programs, and How They Have Changed." *Smile.io*, 14 September 2018, learn.smile.io/blog/a-history-of-loyalty-programs-and-how-they-have-changed
7. Kapp, Karl. *The Gamification of Learning and Instruction*. Wiley, 2012, p. 23
8. Shaw, Jack. "5 Ways to Assess Training Results." *Free Management Library*, 28 September 2011, managementhelp.org/blogs/training-and-development/2011/09/28/5-ways-to-assess-training-results/
9. ATD Research. "Instructional Design Now: A New Age of

Learning and Beyond." *Association for Talent Development*, March 2015, www.td.org/research/instructional-design-now

2. How Much Do You Fail and Play?

1. Sorvino, Chloe. "Inside Billionaire James Dyson's Reinvention Factory: From Vacuums To Hair Dryers And Now Batteries." *Forbes*, 13 September 2016, www.forbes.com/sites/chloesorvino/2016/08/24/james-dyson-exclusive-top-secret-reinvention-factory/#7670f3ab2e87
2. Goodman, Nadia. "James Dyson on Using Failure to Drive Success." *Entrepreneur*, 5 November 2012, www.entrepreneur.com/article/224855
3. Worrall, Simon. "Fun and Games Led to Some of the World's Greatest Inventions." *National Geographic*, 11 December 2016, www.nationalgeographic.com/news/2016/12/wonderland-steven-johnson-play-invention-innovation-design/
4. Brown, Stuart, and Christopher Vaughan. *Play: How it Shapes the Brain, Opens the Imagination, and Invigorates the Soul*. Avery, 2010, p. 145
5. Willis, Judy. "The Neuroscience of Joyful Education." *Engaging the Whole Child,* vol. 64, no. 9, 2007. Retrieved 12 April 2020, from www.ascd.org/publications/educational-leadership/summer07/vol64/num09/The-Neuroscience-of-Joyful-Education.aspx
6. McGonigal, Jane. *Superbetter: The Power of Living Gamefully*. Penguin Books, 2016, p. 30-36
7. Ibid, p. 47
8. Ibid, p. 117
9. Anderton, Kevin. "Research Report Shows How Much Time We Spend Gaming [Infographic]." *Forbes*, 21 March 2019, www.forbes.com/sites/kevinanderton/2019/03/21/research-report-shows-how-much-time-we-spend-gaming-infographic/#7af6753d3e07
10. Furr, Nathan. "How Failure Taught Edison to Repeatedly Innovate." *Forbes*, 9 August 2011, www.forbes.com/sites/nathanfurr/2011/06/09/how-failure-taught-edison-to-repeatedly-innovate/#4c83d8a265e9.
11. Cohan, Peter. "Proof That Failure Is the Key to Success." *Inc.*, 16 July 2013, www.inc.com/peter-cohan/most-important-key-to-start-up-success-fail-fail.html

12. Resnick, Brian. "The '10,000-hour rule' was debunked again. That's a relief." *Vox,* 23 August 2019, www.vox.com/science-and-health/2019/8/23/20828597/the-10000-hour-rule-debunked
13. Gladwell, Malcolm. *Outliers: Why Some People Succeed and Some Don't.* Little Brown & Co., 2008
14. Cole, Samantha. "Quote Of The Week: Double Your Failure Rate." *Fast Company,* 14 July 2014, www.fastcompany.com/3033003/quote-of-the-week-double-your-failure-rate

3. Thinking Errors

1. Madrigal, Alexis. "Old, Weird Tech: The Bat Bombs of World War II." *The Atlantic,* 14 April 2011, www.theatlantic.com/technology/archive/2011/04/old-weird-tech-the-bat-bombs-of-world-war-ii/237267/; Giaimo, Cara. "The Almost Perfect World War II Plot To Bomb Japan With Bats." *Atlas Obscura,* 5 August 2015, www.atlasobscura.com/articles/the-almost-perfect-world-war-ii-plot-to-bomb-japan-with-bats; Neer, Robert. "Behind the Lines- Bats Out of Hell." *History.net,* Retrieved from www.historynet.com/behind-lines-bats-hell.htm
2. Stromberg, Joseph. "B.F. Skinner's Pigeon-Guided Rocket." *Smithsonian Magazine,* 18 August 2011, www.smithsonianmag.com/smithsonian-institution/bf-skinners-pigeon-guided-rocket-53443995/
3. Wallis, Claudia. "To err is human - and a powerful prelude to learning." *The Hechinger Report,* 26 July 2017, hechingerreport.org/getting-errors-all-wrong/
4. Friedman, Susan. "Tsk, No, Eh-eh: Clearing the Path to Reinforcement with an Errorless Learning Mindset." Animal Behavior Management Alliance Conference, 18-22 April 2016, Tampa, FL. Retrieved from www.behaviorworks.org/files/articles/Errorless%20Learning.pdf
5. Metcalfe, Janet. "Learning from Errors." *Annual Review of Psychology,* vol. 68:465-489, 2017.doi.org/10.1146/annurev-psych-010416-044022
6. Ibid.
7. Kapur, Manu & Katerine Bielaczyc. "Designing for Productive Failure." *Journal of the Learning Sciences,* vol.21, no. 1, 2012, p. 45-83. Retrieved from www.tandfonline.com/doi/abs/10.1080/10508406.2011.591717

NOTES

8. Eva, Amy. "Why We Should Embrace Mistakes in School." *Greater Good Magazine*, 28 November 2017, greatergood.berkeley.edu/article/item/why_we_should_embrace_mistakes_in_school

9. Stevenson, Harold, and James Stigler. *The Learning Gap: Why Our Schools Are Failing and What We Can Learn from Japanese and Chinese Education.* Simon & Schuster, 2006, p. 194

10. Eva, Amy. "Why We Should Embrace Mistakes in School." *Greater Good Magazine*, 28 November 2017, greatergood.berkeley.edu/article/item/why_we_should_embrace_mistakes_in_school

11. Press Association. "Children in East Asian Countries Best at Maths - Followed by Northern Ireland." *The Daily Mail*, 29 November 2016, www.dailymail.co.uk/wires/pa/article-3981826/Children-East-Asian-countries-best-maths--followed-Northern-Ireland.html

12. Meyer, Stephen. "Design Tip: Productive Failure." *Learning Solutions*, 8 January 2015, learningsolutionsmag.com/articles/1599/design-tip-productive-failure

13. Metcalfe, Janet. "Learning from Errors." *Annual Review of Psychology*, vol. 68:465-489, 2017.doi.org/10.1146/annurev-psych-010416-044022

14. Schroder, Hans, et al. "Kids Should Pay More Attention To Mistakes, Study Suggests." *Research@MSU*, research.msu.edu/kids-should-pay-more-attention-to-mistake-study-suggests/

15. Casuto, Simon. "Why Failure Is The Key To Workplace Culture Success." *Forbes*, 27 July 2016, www.forbes.com/sites/theyec/2016/07/27/why-failure-is-the-key-to-workplace-culture-success/#648bb5f648f4

16. Question source: BRiddles. "Number Sequence Puzzles With Answers: Best Riddles and Brain Teasers." *BRiddles*, Retrieved 12 April 2020, from www.briddles.com/riddles/number-sequence

17. Question source: Gardner, Martin. "Top 10 Martin Gardner Physics Stumpers." *Martin Gardner Centennial*, Retrieved 12 April 2020, from martin-gardner.org/Top10MGPhysics.html

18. Eva, Amy. "Why We Should Embrace Mistakes in School." *Greater Good Magazine*, 28 November 2017, greatergood.berkeley.edu/article/item/why_we_should_embrace_mistakes_in_school

19. Metcalfe, Janet. "Learning from Errors." *Annual Review of Psychology*, vol. 68:465-489, 2017.doi.org/10.1146/annurev-psych-010416-044022

4. Failing Fast and Cheap

1. Zhang, Maggie. "The Founder Of FedEx Saved The Company From Bankruptcy With His Blackjack Winnings." *Business Insider*, 16 July 2014, www.businessinsider.com/fedex-saved-from-bankruptcy-with-blackjack-winnings-2014-7
2. "Why We Care More About Losses Than Gains." *Morning Edition*. NPR, 25 October 2013. Retrieved from www.npr.org/templates/story/story.php?storyId=240685257
3. Richards, Carl. "Overcoming an Aversion to Loss." *The New York Times*, 9 December 2013, www.nytimes.com/2013/12/09/your-money/overcoming-an-aversion-to-loss.html
4. Wergin, Jon. *Deep Learning in a Disorienting World*. Cambridge University Press, 2019, p. 167
5. Kelland, Kate. "Brain study finds what eases pain of financial loss." *Reuters*, 21 February 2012, www.reuters.com/article/us-brain-financial-loss/brain-study-finds-what-eases-pain-of-financial-loss-idUSTRE81K0GS20120221
6. Genauck, Alexander, et al. "Reduced loss aversion in pathological gambling and alcohol dependence is associated with differential alterations in amygdala and prefrontal functioning." *Scientific Reports,* vol. 7:16306, 2017. Retrieved from doi.org/10.1038/s41598-017-16433-y
7. Walton, Alice. "Why The Brains Of High-Powered People May Be More Prone To Addiction." *Forbes,* 6 August 2013, www.forbes.com/sites/alicegwalton/2013/08/06/why-the-brains-of-high-powered-people-may-be-more-prone-to-addiction/#537fe79d3736
8. Three quotes on failing fast and cheap come from: Saujani, Reshma. Quoted in *Founder Mantras*, 9 February 2016. Retrieved from foundermantras.com/2016-02-09; Feyman, Richard. Quoted in Clegg, Brian, and Paul Birch. *Crash Course in Creativity*. Kogan Page, 2002, p. 7; Hoffman, Reid. Quoted in Saint, Nick. "If You're Not Embarrassed By The First Version Of Your Product, You've Launched Too Late." *Business Insider*, 13 November 2009, www.businessinsider.com/the-iterate-fast-and-release-often-philosophy-of-entrepreneurship-2009-11
9. Paul, Annie. "Researchers Find That Frequent Tests Can Boost Learning." *Scientific American*, 1 August 2015, www.scientificamerican.com/article/researchers-find-that-frequent-tests-can-boost-learning/

NOTES

10. Carey, Benedict. *How We Learn: The Surprising Truth About When, Where and Why It Happens.* Random House, 2015, p. 187. Emphasis mine.
11. Ibid, p. 188
12. Ibid, p. 191-192

5. Die Trying

1. Crawley, Dan. "42 Dark Souls II players die every second - and nine other chilling stats." *Venture Beat*, 25 April 2014, venturebeat.com/2014/04/25/42-dark-souls-ii-players-die-every-second-and-nine-other-chilling-stats/
2. Harbison, Cammy. "'Minecraft Hardcore' streamer loses 5-year world record in a most unfortunate way." *Newsweek*, 30 April 2019, www.newsweek.com/minecraft-hardcore-world-record-broken-philza-phil-watson-death-five-year-run-1410286
3. Thompson, Clive. "The Joy of Sucking." *Wired*, 17 July 2006, www.wired.com/2006/07/the-joy-of-sucking/
4. Sparks, Matt. "Metafocus: Well-designed Failure in Serious Games." *Learning Solutions*, 26 September 2019, learningsolutionsmag.com/articles/metafocus-well-designed-failure-in-serious-games
5. Eva, Amy. "Why We Should Embrace Mistakes in School." *Greater Good Magazine*, 28 November 2017, greatergood.berkeley.edu/article/item/why_we_should_embrace_mistakes_in_school
6. Teach Thought Staff. "How To Help Your Students Embrace Failure Through Game-Based Learning." *Teach Thought*, 4 March 2019, www.teachthought.com/learning/help-students-embrace-failure-game-based-learning/
7. Bowen, Lisa. "Video game play may provide learning, health, social benefits, review finds." *American Psychological Association,* vol. 45, no. 2, 2014.www.apa.org/monitor/2014/02/video-game
8. Gray, Peter. "Benefits of Play Revealed in Research on Video Gaming." *Psychology Today*, 17 March 2018, www.psychologytoday.com/us/blog/freedom-learn/201803/benefits-play-revealed-in-research-video-gaming?amp
9. Juul, Jesper. *The Art of Failure: An Essay on the Pain of Playing Video Games.* MIT Press, 2016, p. 21. Emphasis mine.
10. Corbett, Sara. "Learning by Playing: Video Games in the

Classroom." *The New York Times*, 15 September 2010, www.nytimes.com/2010/09/19/magazine/19video-t.html
11. Toppo, Greg. *The Game Believes in You: How Digital Play Can Make Our Kids Smarter*. Palgrave Macmillan Trade, 2015, p. 5
12. Klein, Christopher. "10 Things You May Not Know About Babe Ruth." *History*, 22 August 2018, www.history.com/news/10-things-you-may-not-know-about-babe-ruth
13. Patel, Sujan. "7 Lessons on Failure You Can Learn From Top Athletes." *Entrepreneur*, 9 October 2017, www.entrepreneur.com/article/300699
14. Landers, Chris. "Every Perfect Game in Major League History, Ranked." *MLB.com*, 19 July 2017, www.mlb.com/cut4/ranking-the-best-perfect-games-in-mlb-history-c242688846; "Major League Baseball & MLB Encyclopedia." *Baseball Reference*, www.baseball-reference.com/leagues/index.shtml

6. Obstacles and Magic Circles

1. Juul, Jesper. *The Art of Failure: An Essay on the Pain of Playing Video Games*. MIT Press, 2016, p. 12. Emphasis mine.
2. Suits, Bernard. Quoted in McGonigal, Jane. *Superbetter: The Power of Living Gamefully*. Penguin Books, 2016, p. 144-145
3. Kelley, Michael. "Here's Robin Williams' Unforgettable Joke About The Invention Of Golf From His Grammy-Winning Broadway Performance (NSFW)." *Business Insider*, 12 August 2014, www.businessinsider.com/robin-williams-on-golf-2014-8. For a video of Williams' performance, visit https://youtu.be/pcnFbCCgTo4
4. Huizinga, Johan. *Homo Ludens*. Routledge & Kegan Paul, 1949, p. 10. Retrieved 12 April 2020, from art.yale.edu/file_columns/0000/1474/homo_ludens_johan_huizinga_routledge_1949_.pdf
5. Salen, Katie, and Eric Zimmerman. *Rules of Play: Game Design Fundamentals*. MIT Press, 2003, p. 51. Zimmerman also uses a similar example of a board game to describe the transformation from decorative set piece to the center of a magic circle once people decide to play.
6. Behling, Steve. *Spider-Man Into the Spider-verse: The Junior Novel*. Little, Brown and Company, 2018

NOTES

7. Salen, Katie, and Eric Zimmerman. *Rules of Play: Game Design Fundamentals*. MIT Press, 2003, p. 304
8. Ogrodnik, Irene. "Athletes helping rival athletes: 5 examples of true sportsmanship." *Global News*, 14 February 2014, globalnews.ca/news/1144378/athletes-helping-rival-athletes-5-examples-of-true-sportsmanship/
9. Juul, Jesper. *The Art of Failure: An Essay on the Pain of Playing Video Games*. MIT Press, 2016, p. 85

7. The First Step to Gamifying

1. Keats, Alex. "Why Large Rewards Programs Failed and What You Can Learn From Them." *Smile.io*, 25 July 2017, learn.smile.io/blog/why-large-rewards-programs-failed-and-what-you-can-learn-from-them
2. *The Bulwer Lytton Fiction Contest*. Retrieved 12 April 2020, from www.bulwer-lytton.com/. The 2019 Bulwer Lytton Fiction Contest Winner was Maxwell Archer for this first sentence of a novel: *"Space Fleet Commander Brad Brad sat in silence, surrounded by a slowly dissipating cloud of smoke, maintaining the same forlorn frown that had been fixed upon his face since he'd accidentally destroyed the phenomenon known as time, thirteen inches ago."*
3. "All About Steve (2009)." *Rotten Tomatoes*. Retrieved 12 April 2020, from www.rottentomatoes.com/m/all_about_steve
4. Marikar, Sheila. "Sandra Bullock Wins Both Best and Worst Actress." *ABC News*, 7 March 2010, abcnews.go.com/Entertainment/Oscars/sandra-bullock-wins-awards-worst-best-actress-weekend/story?id=10038093
5. Metcalfe, Janet. "Learning from Errors." *Annual Review of Psychology*, vol. 68:465-489, 2017.doi.org/10.1146/annurev-psych-010416-044022
6. Carse, James. *Finite and Infinite Games*. The Free Press, 2013
7. "Gridiron Guts: The Story of Football's Carlisle Indians." *Weekend Edition*. NPR, 19 May 2007. Retrieved from www.npr.org/templates/story/story.php?storyId=10217979
8. Trex, Ethan. "5 Things You Didn't Know About Glenn 'Pop' Warner." *Mental Floss*, 6 August 2010, www.mentalfloss.com/article/25404/5-things-you-didnt-know-about-glenn-pop-warner
9. Brown, Stuart, and Christopher Vaughan. *Play: How it Shapes the*

Brain, Opens the Imagination, and Invigorates the Soul. Avery, 2010, p. 214

10. McGonigal, Jane. *Superbetter: The Power of Living Gamefully.* Penguin Books, 2016, p. 14
11. Shout out to my friend Joe, who pointed out that an endnote is the perfect place to hide an Easter egg.
12. Stuart, Keith. "The 12 greatest video game 'Easter eggs.'" *The Guardian,* 2 April 2015, www.theguardian.com/technology/2015/apr/02/12-greatest-video-game-easter-eggs
13. Brown, Stuart, and Christopher Vaughan. *Play: How it Shapes the Brain, Opens the Imagination, and Invigorates the Soul.* Avery, 2010, p. 206
14. Bartle, Richard. "Hearts, Clubs, Diamonds, Spades: Players Who Suit MUDs." *Journal of MUD Research,* vol. 1, no. 1, 1996. Retrieved 12 April 2020, from mud.co.uk/richard/hcds.htm.
15. Juul, Jesper. *The Art of Failure: An Essay on the Pain of Playing Video Games.* MIT Press, 2016, p. 68
16. American Physical Society. "This Month in Physics History." *APS Physics,* July 2013. Retrieved 12 April 2020, from www.aps.org/publications/apsnews/201307/physicshistory.cfm
17. *Clay Mathematics Institute.* "The Millennium Prize Problems." Retrieved 12 April 2020, from www.claymath.org/millennium-problems/millennium-prize-problems
18. Question Sources: en.wikipedia.org/wiki/Mr._Potato_Head; www.history.com/news/how-long-was-the-hundred-years-war; www.ascentoftheamazon.com/learning-resources/rivers-tributaries/; www.rd.com/culture/last-letter-added-to-the-alphabet/; www.sciencealert.com/why-are-venus-and-uranus-spinning-in-the-wrong-direction; Retrieved 12 April 2020.

9. The Playing Human

1. Miyamoto, Shigeru. Quoted in Mäyrä, Frans. *An Introduction to Game Studies.* SAGE, 2008, p. 75
2. Koster, Raph. *A Theory of Fun for Game Design.* Paraglyph Press, 2005, p. 60
3. Huizinga, Johan. *Homo Ludens.* Routledge & Kegan Paul, 1949. Quote appears in page one of Foreword. Retrieved 12 April 2020, from art.yale.edu/file_columns/0000/1474/homo_ludens_johan_huizinga_routledge_1949_.pdf

Manufactured by Amazon.ca
Bolton, ON